EMBRACING
FEAR

EMBRACING
FEAR

How to Turn What Scares Us into Our Greatest Gift

THOM RUTLEDGE

HarperSanFrancisco

FIRST HARPERCOLLINS PAPERBACK EDITION PUBLISHED IN 2005

Library of Congress Cataloging-in-Publication Data is available.
ISBN-13: 978–0–06–251755–3
ISBN-10: 0–06–251775–9

05 06 07 08 09 QM 10 9 8 7 6 5 4 3 2 1

In loving and grateful memory of
Charles Leon Smith, Jr.
1918–2001
and
Antoinette McDonald Smith
1919–2001
real-life heroes and
authentic role models
of genuine courage

If I refuse to listen to the voice of fear,
would the voice of courage whisper in my ear?
—JANA STANFIELD, Brave Faith

Contents

In day-to-day life, you can quickly tell the difference between the two. Imagine, for example, you're about to board a flight and you're suddenly overtaken with dread and uncertainty about the pilot's ability to fly the plane. If that dread is based on a plane crash you saw on the news three weeks ago, it is unwarranted fear. If the fear is based upon seeing the pilot stumble out of the airport bar, it's the real thing.

True fear is the messenger that intuition sends when the situation is urgent, and it's not easily quieted. If you want it to leave you alone, whatever questions it poses must be answered. Thom helps us find those answers. He's a funny, compassionate teacher whose class could be called Fear 101—or more intelligently I suppose, Embracing Fear.

Thom shows us the power we gain when we stand up to fear—and the bullies who deliver it. Governments have embraced fear, but in a much different way than Thom suggests. Throughout history governments have used fear as the perfect method for persuading (and often bullying) populations to accept actions they might otherwise resist. All governments on earth want their citizens to believe that only the government can protect them, and they know this works best if they generate fears that are new and improved. The old fears just don't get our attention as well.

The fear du jour for both the government and the news media, as if you need a reminder, is terrorism—but it's always something. It's as if there's a space in our collective mind reserved for things that frighten us, and that space must be kept occupied. If we are not fearing terrorism, it's mad cow disease, or killer bees, or gas-tank fires, or dangerous tires. Before September 11, we feared enemies within: AIDS, asbestos, the vengeful coworker, the local serial killer, the home invasion robber, the rampaging high-school student.

A scientific poll conducted before 9/11 asked Americans what they feared, revealing a virtual catalogue of catastrophes right off the television news. About a fifth of the respondents reported a fear being in an air crash.

This isn't surprising given that, through the magic of video, we are there whenever a plane falls to earth, wherever on earth that happens to happen. So there are people who drive to the airport obsessing about their plane crashing even as they do something far riskier than flying: drive without paying attention.

While 20 percent of Americans were worried about being in an air crash, 18 percent worried they'd become victims of mass violence. The two fears collided on 9/11, so, while the percentages of fearful people would be higher today, my point is that these fears are not new.

Even before 9/11, there were people who'd cancel a trip to see the pyramids in Egypt for fear of being killed by terrorists, and then stay in Detroit—where the risk of homicide is twenty times greater!

One in three Americans fears being a victim of a violent crime, even though only one in one hundred and fifty actually will be. This fear of being harmed by other people is understandable (though often misplaced), but what about the fear of electromagnetic fields (16 percent of Americans), or the fear of foreign viruses (30 percent)? I actually met a lady with that fear, by the way. Where? In a television news studio, of course. The station was doing a special segment on a lethal new disease virtually certain to kill us all before the end of sweeps week. It was a scary sounding, hard to ignore, got-to-see-this, "Honey, get in here!" made-for-TV disease. As you may have already guessed, it was the flesh-eating disease. Lacking anyone who actually suffered from the malady, television officials brought in a woman who was worried that she might have it. I was introduced to her before she headed to the studio, and as I watched her interview, it crossed my mind that she could have told me all this before shaking my hand. But no matter, she didn't have it, and I didn't catch it, and neither will you.

What's left to fear? Well, more than a third of Americans fear getting food poisoning from meat, a fear as rich in irony as meat is rich in cholesterol, because uncontaminated or "safe" meat contributes to many more deaths than does food poisoning each year.

When I think like this (you know, reasonably), I hear the words of the television news producer in Chicago who assured me that "A little worry never hurt anybody," and that is just not so. Through high blood pressure, heart disease, depression, addiction, and a myriad of other stress-related ailments, anxiety kills more Americans each year than all the foreign viruses, bad meat, electromagnetic fields, and airplane crashes put together .

Think of the times your mind just wouldn't stop chewing on something, just couldn't stop tossing and turning on its own bed of nails, just couldn't find peace. Television news is that exact same mental energy given a billion dollars in resources, inspired to dwell on every fear, wired to propel itself far and near, spinning around the world until it reaches terminal velocity.

The news media is a giant mind, a giant unquiet, over-stimulated mind that won't let itself rest—and won't let the rest of us rest either.

In millions of homes, newscasters are guests who arrive

in the afternoon full of frightening tales and gory pictures. They stay through dinner, enthusiastically adding grisly details that make the kids wince, and they're still around at bedtime to recite a scary story or two. While newscasters are showing slides of thier awful vacation, you slump to sleep, only to find in the morning that they are still there, eager and fast talking, following you around the kitchen warning you about the dangers of coffee.

Little wonder we Americans are steeped in anxiety and unwarranted fear: having lived through the previously unthinkable, our minds are more open to the unfathomable—and television news has rushed through that opening. We are built to anticipate what's coming next, and television feeds this natural interest with stories about things that aren't actually coming next: worst-case scenarios and dark predictions delivered by presentable-looking "experts" who validate our wildest worries. Footage from past disasters is mixed with scary graphics; in all the confusion, the qualifying words (might, allegedly, possibly, could, potentially, conceivably) drop from consciousness, leaving only the sense that danger is everywhere around us. Combine the words, the graphics, the logos, the music, the urgency and you end up with a small amount of information hidden behind an unhealthy dose of sensation—and the sensation is fear.

Since there can't be a video of what isn't happening, television news producers show us terrifying footage of some other incident. They call someone a "nuclear terrorism expert," which is an unusual expertise considering there's never been an act of nuclear terrorism.

With all the risk and danger television sprays at us each day like tear gas, it occurs to me they should simply open

each evening's show by saying, "Welcome to the Channel
Two News; we're very surprised you made it through
another day."

We can really use Thom's help with all this, particularly
given that fully 90 percent of Americans feel less safe today
than they did growing up. But let's take a look at that
"safer" world of your youth. It was a world without airbags
or mandatory seatbelts, before the decrease in smoking,
before early detection of cancer was possible, before 911
systems showed dispatchers the addresses of people in distress. You remember those carefree fifties before CAT
scans, ultrasound, organ transplants, amniocentesis, and
coronary bypass surgery. Remember those oh-so-safe sixties
when angry world powers struck war-like postures and
schoolchildren practiced monthly air-raid drills on how to
survive nuclear attack?

The fact is that young people are more likely to survive
childhood today than in 1960. Vehicle fatalities have
dropped 25 percent since then, deaths by other accidents
have been cut in half, and cancer deaths have been reduced
by 30 percent.

Admittedly, the violence we see today is far more grue-
some than what we saw growing up—but that's the point:
it's the violence we see. We have a far larger catalogue of
fears to draw upon, and I believe we'll all be safer (and of
course happier) if we throw that catalogue out with the
other junk mail.

The book you're holding can help you do that.

With fear, as with physics, everything we give energy to
takes energy from something else. Thus, needless worry has
several costs. My suggestion is to explore every intuitive sig-

nal (of which fear is one), but do so briefly and not repetitively. When faced with some worry or uncertain fear, ask yourself the following: Am I responding to something in my environment or to something in my imagination? Is this feeling based on something I perceive in my circumstance, or merely something in my memory?

If the feeling is a worry, we just chew on it, giving the illusion that we're doing something, when in fact, worry is stalling us from doing something. Conversely, when a dreaded outcome is actually imminent, we don't worry about it—we take action. Seeing lava from the local volcano ooze down the street toward our house does not cause any worry; it causes running.

The best antidote to worry is action. Hence, if there's an action that will lessen the likelihood of a dreaded outcome occurring, and if that action doesn't cost too much in terms of effort or freedom, then take it. The worry about whether we remembered to close the baby gate at the top of the stairs can be stopped in an instant by checking. Then it isn't a worry anymore; it's just a brief impulse. Almost all worry evolves from the conflict between intuition and inaction.

My work has focused on fear of violence and death, but of course, those aren't the only fears that hold us back. After all, everybody dies, but not everybody lives. I'm confident this book will help many people to really live. As Thom teaches, "Sometimes fear is part of the problem. Sometimes fear is the problem." When we are really paying attention, he says, fear can also be part of the solution.

We're funny creatures who can always find some fear or worry to get in our way. For example, without the help of

CHAPTER ONE

Don't Run, Don't Hide
The Power of Fear

There is only one freedom: the freedom from fear.
—ORIAH MOUNTAIN DREAMER

WE ALL KNOW FEAR. I'm not talking just about the big fears—terror and panic—but fear in all its variations. Fear is our constant companion, our day-to-day nemesis, and our ultimate challenge.

Fear fuels our negative and judgmental thoughts and our need to control things. Fear underlies guilt and shame and anger. Every difficult emotion we experience represents some kind of threat—a threat to our self-esteem or to the stability of a relationship (personal or professional), even to our right to be alive. And threat translates to fear. Start with any difficult emotion you choose, get on the elevator, press *B* for basement, and there, below the guilt and shame and anger, below the negativity and the judgments, you will find it: fear.

Fear hides inside seemingly less severe emotions such as anxiety, worry, and nervousness, each of which has various levels and shadings. The objects of anxiety can range from giving a presentation at work to the presence of terrorism in our world. We can worry that our shoes don't match an outfit or worry about larger concerns like world hunger. We can be somewhat nervous about performing at a recital or seriously nervous about the results of an HIV test.

Although fear is a major influence in every one of our lives, it is not always negative. As we will discuss at length, fear is essentially a positive mechanism, an ingenious natural design to keep us safe. And there are plenty of opportunities for that healthy fear to work its magic, guiding us this way and that, alerting us to danger and aligning us with what is good and right in the world.

But our big human brains have created a spin-off design. The new design is a fear we can self-impose without need of external causes. "No, thank you," we say. "I don't need any real danger to activate my fear. I can do it perfectly well myself." Or we can take any legitimate fear and work with it until we are paralyzed, barely able to get a decent breath. What an excellent job we do wasting our valuable mental energy like this.

On January 6, 1941, at a time in history when considerable legitimate fear was in the air, Franklin Delano Roosevelt gave a speech to the U.S. Congress. World War II was brewing, but the United States had not yet joined the fight; the Japanese would not attack Pearl Harbor for another eleven months. President Roosevelt spoke with courage about protecting lives and a way of life:

> In future days, which we seek to make secure, we look forward to a world founded upon four essential human freedoms.
>
> The first is freedom of speech and expression—everywhere in the world.
>
> The second is freedom of every person to worship God in his own way—everywhere in the world.
>
> The third is freedom from want—which, translated into world terms, means economic understandings which will secure to every nation a healthy peacetime life for its inhabitants—everywhere in the world.
>
> The fourth is freedom from fear—which, translated into world terms, means a worldwide reduction of armaments to such a point and in such a thorough fashion that no nation will be in a position to commit an act of physical aggression against any neighbor—anywhere in the world.

President Roosevelt also said that a world based on these four freedoms was "no vision of a distant millennium," but "a definite basis for a kind of world attainable in our own time and generation."

In the sixty years since the "four freedoms" speech, we have experienced times of relative peace, mostly continuing conflict and political turbulence, and we have experienced dangers beyond what Mr. Roosevelt could have imagined. It would never have occurred to him, for instance, that there would be a time when a small knife or box cutter in the hands of a terrorist would be enough armament to transform a domestic airliner into a deadly guided missile.

Unfortunately we have not manifested the world of freedoms President Roosevelt envisioned, and as we stand in that distant millennium we long for such a world perhaps more than ever. The countless political explanations for this are beyond the scope of my expertise and of this book, but as a psychotherapist I do believe I have something to contribute here, something to say about how we might still rationally hope to live in a world free of fear.

When Franklin Roosevelt delineated the four freedoms, the fourth being the freedom from fear, he was specifically referring to our right to live without fear of external threat of war and destruction. My work as a psychotherapist has been largely about how to claim our right to live without fear of internal war and destruction. I have spent thousands of hours in conversation with people—individually and in groups—working to increase understanding and solve problems. I couldn't possibly recall all of the various strategies, techniques, and philosophies I have enlisted toward these ends, but I can report that no matter what the approach, in every single difficulty I have encountered—mine or someone else's—fear has been involved.

Sometimes fear is part of the problem. Sometimes fear *is* the problem. And when we are really paying attention, fear is usually part of the solution. Fear is an essential part of our nature, installed in our DNA, no doubt for very good reason.

Fear is an alarm system. It is there to get our attention, to push us in one direction or another, out of harm's way. Fear is not pathological; it is part of our intelligence, part of an ingenious guidance system to help ensure our survival—as individuals, as communities, and as a species.

How we face and respond to our individual personal fears is integrally related to how we respond as communities, as nations, and as a species to the external threats that we have faced, that we face now, and that we have yet to face. I believe that when we make the decision to stand and face our individual demons, we are contributing to the potential for peace throughout the world. The ripples emanating from our individual efforts to grow may be small, but they are there. You cannot drop a pebble in the pond without creating a ripple effect. The personal-growth work you do is the pebble in the pond, creating its own ripple effect. How you treat your family, friends, and even the person standing next to you in the supermarket line are your pebbles in the pond. Maybe Roosevelt's vision of a world characterized by the four freedoms is still a possibility. If so, I am sure that it begins with facing our own fears.

We must emphasize this from the very beginning: our natural mechanism of fear is not the problem. We have used our higher intelligence to create a monster out of what is essentially a healthy, natural response to adverse or potentially dangerous situations. This book is not about how to be rid of that monster, but rather how to live beyond its tyrannical control. This book will guide you to clearly identify the voices within your mind (be assured, we all have them), and it will

give you a game plan, including specific techniques, to help
you distinguish between healthy and unhealthy fear. The
short version, the simple-but-not-so-easy, sound-bite version
of this book is this:

> Separate the voices of healthy and unhealthy fear.
> Listen carefully to and follow the wise counsel of the
>   healthy fear.
> Tell the unhealthy fear to sit down and shut up.

Of course if it were that easy you would not be reading
and I would not have written this book.

It is essential that we begin by differentiating between
healthy and unhealthy fear. The anxieties and worries that
pervade our daily lives—the real troublemakers—are not
born from healthy fear, but from neurotic fear. Healthy fear
stands guard responsibly, informing us immediately of real
danger. Neurotic fear works around the clock, exaggerating
and even inventing potential dangers. Healthy fear is about
protection and guidance. Neurotic fear is about the need to
be in control. Healthy fear inspires us to do what can be
done in the present. Neurotic fear speaks to us endlessly
about everything that could possibly go wrong tomorrow, or
the next day, or next year.

As you read on, I encourage you to personify each of
these, creating specific human images to characterize your
healthy fear and your neurotic fear. See them as two advisors, each with his own personality and agenda. By referring
to fear with the masculine pronoun, my intention is to be as

accurate as possible, not sexist. The overwhelming majority of clients and workshop participants, including women, with whom I have used this metaphor have instantly identified their fear as male. My personal opinion is that this is a reflection of a male-dominated society and is not a particularly positive reflection on my gender as a whole. For the purposes of this book, I will refer to fear as male, so as to avoid the cumbersome, repetitive "he or she," and because I do not believe that we can achieve the degree of personification of neurotic fear that we need if we take the neutral path of referring to fear as "it." What is most important for this work is that we see and hear fear as a person. Whether your fear is male or female is of less importance. Feel free to make the adjustment as you read if your fear is female.

The ability to perceive ourselves "in relationship" to our fears, rather than identified with or even possessed by them, is the single most powerful technique I have ever discovered to help overcome the control that neurotic fear imposes in our lives. This book will teach you how to identify, understand, and change your relationship with your fear. I strongly recommend that you practice this technique to the point of mastery. It can make all the difference in how you face the good in life and how you face what is genuinely scary.

Nothing in this book will hinder the functioning of your healthy fear. To do so would be irresponsible, compromising your ability to respond effectively to the very real circumstances of your life. If you sustain a head injury and go to your local hospital emergency room, the medical staff there will not administer medication for your pain until they are

certain of an accurate diagnosis and proper treatment plan.
Their refusal to rescue you from the pain is not sadistic, and
not even because your HMO has not preapproved pain medication in the event of head trauma on a Wednesday afternoon. They will not medicate the pain of a head injury
because to do so would interfere with their gathering of
essential information that could save your life. The pain is
the source of that information. Likewise, healthy fear is a
valuable source of information for each of us, and we are
well advised to follow the emergency-room model, opting to
pay close attention to the fear, rather than dulling it or distracting ourselves from it.

This book will teach you to identify and accept guidance
from your healthy fear, and it will teach you how to stand up
to and move beyond the toxic control of neurotic fear. To
begin learning the important distinction between the two,
consider the following scenario.

You sit in an office with two advisors. Healthy fear is the
strong, silent type, he assures you that he will remain vigilant, ready to inform you of real dangers as they come into
view. This advisor will not expend valuable energy dreaming
up and telling you about every conceivable possible danger,
imagining the innumerable ways things could go wrong.
Further, your healthy-fear advisor tells you that each report
of real danger will be accompanied by reasonable recommendations about the intensity and timing of your response. For
instance, the fear that will motivate you to jump out of the
way of an oncoming bus will be quite different from the fear
of not living up to a particular expectation you have of your-

self. And the fear you experience when being told you are at risk for heart disease will be different still. When you are in the path of the bus, healthy fear will not suggest that you remember to get a bus schedule the next chance you get, so that you can avoid being run over in the future. And when you are afraid you have not lived up to your potential in a professional or personal situation, this advisor will not recommend that you go stand in the path of an oncoming bus.

Healthy fear, it seems, will sort through and handle a tremendous amount of complex information, but the recommended responses will remain as simple and efficient as possible. If the bus is approaching, get the hell out of the street. If you have an unexplained, persistent pain, make an appointment with the doctor.

Neurotic fear, on the other hand, is anything but silent. This advisor talks nonstop, pointing out every conceivable potential danger, small, medium, and large. This advisor suggests a rather steady anxiety—tightness in your chest, butterflies in your stomach—in response to everything from the potential of the deadly bus to the possibility that the person you met two days ago might not like you. This advisor, your neurotic fear, paces the floor while talking, doesn't sit down, and doesn't shut up. The very presence of this advisor makes you extremely nervous. Your neurotic-fear advisor constantly reminds you of potential negative outcomes. The philosophy here seems to be, "If something could go wrong, let's focus on it." When confronted with any success, neurotic fear remains unshaken. He has the ability to stand in the midst of quite positive progress and continue to recite negative prophecies, spouting off threats: "If you do [fill in the blank], you'll be sorry." "What makes you think you could ever [again, fill in the blank]?"

For many of us, neurotic fear shows up early in life. My earliest memory of neurotic fear is the dread that filled me when I successfully completed fourth grade (with straight A's). Rather than feeling happy or proud of my accomplishment, I was convinced I would certainly reach my limit of competence and not be able to do "fifth-grade work." Neurotic fear prefers to deal in extremes. I don't recall being afraid that I might be a little unprepared for the next test or for fifth grade; I was always afraid of absolute failure. As I sit listening to my two advisors, I notice that neurotic fear has not changed a bit: he loves to predict total disaster.

The scenario continues. You sit behind your desk listening to and considering these two very different advisors. You look back and forth between the strong, silent one and the constantly chattering, constantly moving, highly agitated one, who still talks even when you are no longer listening. You consider them both for a moment. After a very short amount of time, giving it almost no thought, you put the second advisor—the neurotic, agitated, fretful doomsday prophet—in charge of your life.

If having this kind of meeting between multiple characters in your mind makes you at all uneasy, be assured that these inner conversations are not evidence of insanity, but the product of normal human consciousness.

One important goal of this book is to teach you to move past what I call the "myth of singularity"—the belief that we are supposed to have only one opinion and one feeling at a time—to a more realistic and effective frame of reference for thinking about your relationship to fear. Specifically, we will look at why and how we as otherwise intelligent human beings can look at the glaring contrast between healthy and neurotic fear, and in spite of what is rational and wise consistently choose neurotic fear as our lead advisor.

Most people will recognize these two advisors. Some of us may say we know them intimately—especially the neurotic fear, the one my wife calls the "Bully" and one of my clients calls the "Chairman." This scenario, in which you put the clearly least-qualified character in charge of your life, is funny from a distance, but anything but funny when it is really happening. I want to take you back into that meeting and encourage you to listen carefully to everything being said and to consider all of the implications. I want to show you specifically how to make a different decision, how to fire your neurotic fear from his current position of authority, and how to reinstate healthy fear to its rightful place.

The neurotic fear will tell us that he wants only the best for us. He will never be caught wearing a "Bully" name tag. More likely he shows up claiming to be "the voice of reason," "the realistic one," "your best friend," and sometimes "your only hope."

Healthy fear, the one my wife calls the "Ally," is not pushy. This one is clear, direct, and to the point. The Ally lives within us for one reason only: to protect. The Bully, on the other hand, will claim to protect, and may even intend to protect, but will continually step beyond the bounds of that job description. The Bully overprotects, to the point of control. For many, the Bully's philosophy seems to be: "If I can keep you from taking risks in your life, then you will be saved from hurt, embarrassment, disappointment, and humiliation." The relationship dynamic here is the same as any relationship in which one person dominates another. In such relationships, the "controller" maintains control by promoting a state of perpetual self-doubt. Bottom line: the lower our self-esteem, the easier we are to control. This holds true whether the controlling personality is a parent, a spouse, or a neurotic fear within us.

My intention is not to exaggerate or overdramatize the internal struggle we have with fear. It has been my experience that, although each individual will fall somewhere along the continuum in this matter, to characterize ourselves as "terrorist and hostage all wrapped up in one person" is most often not much of an exaggeration. We quite literally have the unfortunate combination of the capacity and the tendency to terrorize ourselves.

With this book, I hope to challenge you to embark upon a rescue mission. I have discovered, in my own life and in my work with others, that nothing short of life-transforming decisions will do to put us back in charge—or in charge for the first time—of our lives. I want to guide you toward your fear, toward your own Bully, because running away has not worked. I want to show you that the Bully cannot control your life if you do not allow it. And I want to teach you how to not allow it.

As you read, I hope you will pause now and then to identify and differentiate one advisor from the other. You must learn to tell the difference between the Ally and the Bully if you are to make the changes you want to make.

In group therapy—or sometimes in my seminars—I direct a role-playing exercise in which the two advisors sit on either side of a lucky volunteer. After creating a short list of messages for each advisor (specially designed for the volunteer), I instruct both the healthy and the neurotic fears to speak to the person simultaneously. "Don't be polite," I tell the role players. "The voices in our heads aren't. Just keep talking."

Each person's experience with the exercise will of course be unique, but there is definitely a general trend. People sitting between the two advisors usually report trying to listen and stay focused on the Ally (who is saying such things as, "It is important to remain true to yourself," "The thing to fear is not standing up for what you believe in"), but gradually losing the battle, ultimately hearing the Bully's messages clearly and losing awareness of the healthy messages. Not always, but often, the person in the middle will be noticeably leaning toward the Bully by the end of the exercise.

That's what we do: we lean toward the voice of neurotic fear. And we continue to do so even after we have uncovered the more authentic voice of healthy fear. Faced with this choice, how could we possibly continue to take the obviously negative option? Are we that inherently negative? Do we like being afraid all the time? Are we just stupid?

The answer is none of the above. We are not inherently negative, we don't enjoy scaring the hell out of ourselves, and we are not just stupid. Neurotic fear has firmly established itself within our consciousness in two major ways. First, and most simply, the neurotic-fear messages have embedded themselves into our thinking through the years of sheer repetition. And, second, as a natural result of such repetition, the messages have achieved a high level of credibility. They are so familiar that we tend to trust them. In other words, we have been steadily and thoroughly brainwashed by the Bully.

The challenge we face is to reverse that brainwashing, to learn to do more than lean away from the voice of neurotic fear. We must learn to make the conscious choice to turn away from the Bully and toward the Ally. In the group exercise, that is what we do: the person in the middle practices listening to the neurotic fear long enough to identify who and what it is, then he or she is taught to turn away from the Bully and face the Ally. It is still not easy, but with repeated practice and focused attention, the voice of the Ally, with its strength, credibility, and wisdom, begins to assume its rightful place in our consciousness.

In the pages that follow, you will read about some very courageous people who have successfully done this work. And I will tell you about my own work as well. Long ago, I stopped attempting to distinguish between what I know as a mental-health professional and what I know as a human being. I don't think I ever made much of a distinction between my clients and myself, other than to respect our individuality and to remember who was the customer and who was responsible for providing the service. As cliché as this may sound, I believe we are travelers on a common road, or at least travelers whose roads intersect frequently. And it is through the process of sharing our experiences—victories and defeats—with each other that we will find our way to wherever it is we are going.

Please read these pages with a collaborative spirit. I invite you to participate by identifying with what you read and by trying on the ideas, philosophies, and techniques included here. As a frame of reference, consider the following acronym as a map for the journey we are about to take:

Four Steps to Transforming Your Relationship with Fear

- Face it.
- Explore it.
- Accept it.
- Respond to it.

Facing the fear means that we end the running, cringing, and hiding from the scary voice within us, the voice that will always find us no matter where we run or where we hide. *Exploring* it means that we turn and walk toward the big scary Bully. If you think that doesn't take some courage, just wait. *Accepting* it, contrary to popular misconception, does not mean we agree with the fear or that we like it. To accept is simply to realize there are some things we cannot change. The sooner we accept the fact that the scary messages (neurotic fear) running through our minds will not just be erased, the sooner we can move on to investing our valuable energy in the last of these four steps. *Responding* to our neurotic fears is what it is all about, but the ability to change our responses can only be built on the foundation of the first three steps.

When new clients show up in my office for therapy, I want them to expect results. I don't want them to have unrealistic expectations of me or of the process of psychotherapy, but I do want them to believe they will change as a result of the work we will do together.

Personal-growth work—through therapy, seminars, or self-help material—should be collaborative. Never trust someone who presents him- or herself as the ultimate expert on the human condition. I believe I have something significant to share; otherwise I would not sit with clients or write a book. But more important, I believe that any truth you will discover here will be the product of your interaction with what I have to say. The innovative physician/healer Patch Adams points out that we are all doctors and we are all patients. In this same way, we are all teachers and we are all students. I bring what I bring to the table, you bring what you bring, and somewhere in the mix we discover truth.

Jenni is a young woman who has just in the past six months made tremendous progress in her recovery from an eating disorder. She is my favorite kind of client, an enthusiastic, proactive collaborator. She shows up at her sessions ready to fill me in on her progress or lack of progress since our last session, and she always has questions. These are not just rhetorical questions (I wonder why I am having such a hard time? Will I ever get past feeling stuck?); these are questions she wants answered. She doesn't object to the fact that she will very likely have to help me find the answers, but she definitely expects asking questions to lead to discovering answers.

There are different styles of being a client in therapy just as there are different styles of being a therapist. Beyond the obvious choices of personal philosophy, particular school of thought, and specific techniques, style is affected by the personalities of the people involved. Jenni's "client style" is active and energetic. During her sessions, she writes notes into a small, leather-bound notebook and describes what we are doing as writing a self-help book specifically for her. Writing in a journal during personal-growth work can be extremely valuable. A few minutes each day spent recording some of your thoughts and feelings will help to keep you on track during personal-growth work, whether you are attending therapy, participating in support groups, talking to a trusted friend, or just reading this book. Don't worry about being eloquent or organized or having good handwriting. Simply write a few thoughts down. It is a way of sitting down with yourself each day to ask, "How are you doing?" When you sit down and open your journal, you are asking the question; as you write, you are answering. Later, when you read what you have written, you are listening.

I encourage you to give writing a try. You might work with our acronym map by writing, or write position papers from the points of view of each of your advisors, the Ally and the Bully. Or just keep a journal of your thoughts and feelings as you read. I tell therapy clients that keeping a journal can save them time and money because sometimes sitting down with a journal can be as productive as a good therapy session. And as you will see, many of the therapy exercises I describe easily translate into writing exercises.

After giving it a fair chance, if you decide it doesn't fit with your personal style, then let it go. But maybe you will discover, as Jenni has, that you will be writing your own personalized self-help book as you move through this process.

For your sake and mine, please don't expect this book to heal all that ails you. But do take the risk of expecting something of me as the writer and guide and you as the reader and explorer.

However you choose to proceed (there is no wrong way), I absolutely believe that if you are willing to remain open to these ideas and if you are willing to gather and use some new tools as you read, you will change your relationship with your fear. The extent and longevity of that transformation will be purely dependent upon your willingness to put the tools to work in your life on a daily basis.

Some aspects of personal-growth work are exciting: the cathartic release of pent-up emotions, the flash of insight, the comfort and relief that brand-new self-compassion brings. And then there is the hard work, the daily application of what we learn along the way. You must be willing to commit yourself to both the exciting (and scary, of course) and the mundane for any personal-growth material to bear fruit.

I have practiced sleight-of-hand magic with cards since I was a kid, so there are a couple of things I can do with a deck of cards that look pretty easy, but are actually the result of countless hours of repetitive practice. Recently when I was working with Jenni, I suggested she simultaneously practice a particular sleight-of-hand move I have been teaching her and a specific new way of thinking in the sort of stressful situations we have been discussing. I told Jenni that the point of my pairing these two learning challenges is simply this: you should not expect to master a new way of thinking without hours and hours of dedicated practice any more than you would expect to master the card sleight without practice.

I have done my best to include in this book plenty of stories, ideas, and techniques you will be able to use just by reading and doing a little thinking, like magic tricks you can do with minimal rehearsal. But if you will approach *Embracing Fear* with the level of commitment it takes to master a complex card sleight, I know the material included here will help you to transform your life for the better.

Isn't it time you fired the Bully who has been running your life? Isn't it time to put yourself in charge? If considering this scares you, you have come to the right place. Welcome to the ranks of those of us who dare to walk around today believing the ridiculous notion that even though we do not control what might happen, we are in charge of how we will respond, and that the ability to respond is what will determine our level of satisfaction, fulfillment, and even happiness.

When we begin with the first step in our acronym map, *facing the fear,* we put into play what I have come to think of as one of the most underestimated and underappreciated agents of change: awareness. Simply put: darkness is the absence of light; where light shines, there is no darkness; and awareness is that light.

A significant part of what I do for a living is accompany people into their psyches with my trusty flashlight. (I once heard someone say, "My mind is like a bad neighborhood— you don't want to go in there alone.") We shine the beam of light here and there, destroying darkness. The interesting thing about the light of awareness is that once it has revealed something to us, even when the light has gone and the darkness returns, we still know it's there. Once something has been revealed to our conscious minds, we can never return it to the anonymity of total darkness—because we know it's there.

And so it is with fear.

Simple and powerful awareness is the first step to take. As you turn each page of this book, be aware of your fear. Don't run. Don't hide. Don't cover it up with excuses, apologies, self-judgment, or mood-altering chemicals. Move straight toward it. The fear you have spent a lifetime trying to ignore is about to become one of your greatest teachers.

CHAPTER TWO

Stepping Up
The Meaning of "No Fear"

Be just, and fear not.

—WILLIAM SHAKESPEARE

AN INVITATION TO SPEAK at my undergraduate alma mater catapulted me twenty-five years back in time. Two days before, I had attended a seminar in which the question was posed, "If you could travel back in time and you could only make one change, what would it be?" My nostalgic but otherwise ordinary trip to Austin College in Sherman, Texas, was about to provide my answer to that question.

Arriving the night before I was scheduled to give a lecture, I decided to take an evening walk across the college campus where I had spent four of the most important years of my life. With the exception of two or three new buildings, everything seemed basically the same as when I left. What alarmed me was the inescapable feeling that I was basically the same too. I realized I was the same person who had graduated twenty-five years before in one very specific—and not very flattering—way: I was still scared.

In 1972 I had walked across this very same campus as a new college freshman—my hair falling over my shoulders, a red T-shirt worn to a dull pink, faded Levis, and Converse high-tops. On that first day of the fall semester, several of the other new students and sometimes their parents stopped me to ask directions to one building or another. They did not recognize the frightened freshman in me. My fear was not outwardly visible because I had already learned the art of appearing cool and laid back, even when I was actually terrified. For the most part, this ability has served me well; it is an excellent disguise. People have mistaken me for a calm, collected person in the midst of frightening, even chaotic, circumstances all my life. I am happy to report I have made significant progress in becoming genuinely more like that façade, but I still think I frequently appear calmer on the outside than I feel on the inside. It's not my worst habit.

In the fall of 1972 I was externally very calm, in contrast with my internal near panic. So new students and their parents sought my direction. From where I was standing then, there was no way for me to see what I see so clearly today: that this blind-leading-the-blind theme was only just beginning for me.

I lived those college years with enthusiasm, to say the least. I loved feeling independent, but unfortunately I invested my new independence more in the development of my neurosis and alcoholism, than I did in exploring opportunities to fulfill my dream of being a writer. I became increasingly unrealistic in my thinking, alternating between grandiosity—grossly overestimating my talents—and ripping myself to shreds with relentless self-criticism.

In college I taught myself to hide from fear. Alcohol was a good hiding place, as was believing that the success I wanted in life would just magically show up one day. And whether or not self-criticism—self-condemnation, really— hid me from my fear, it provided a way to express it that did me absolutely no good. I don't think I knew I was hiding. I certainly did not understand how afraid I was, and I did not know I was becoming the poster boy for one of fear's greatest supporters: avoidance. I didn't even know who the Bully was, so I could not have known he was already breathing down my neck.

There are dozens of little cards tacked to one wall of my therapy room. I call them "reminders for the therapeutically forgetful." My clients call them "Thom's Nutshells." One of the Nutshells on my wall reads: "Self-Saboteur's Motto: you cannot lose what you do not have." By the time the forty-six-year-old version of me walked across the college campus, I had become a master self-saboteur, but mercifully I had eventually sought help to find my way out of negativity's reign in my life. I had spent years in all kinds of therapy, I was in recovery from alcoholism, and I had even been medically treated for depression. I had done all this, I had helped many others do the same, and I had even fulfilled my dream of being a writer. In short, I had come a long way. But still, as I walked the campus that night, I could not shake the feeling that I had not changed all that much. It didn't make much sense to me, but I could almost hear a little voice within me saying, "Thom, you are still scared."

The little voice—whoever, whatever it was—was not talking about me being a little nervous about the speech I was there to deliver. It was talking about fear being a central, possibly even organizing, element of my very identity. I drifted even farther back in time.

I remembered being afraid as a child—afraid that my parents would die, afraid of the other kids in school, afraid of failing the spelling test, afraid of the "atomic bomb" that could be dropped on us at any moment, afraid of tornadoes. I remembered being afraid as an adolescent—the emerging sense that whatever success I had was fraudulent and the accompanying dread that I would be discovered for the impostor I was. (This so-called impostor syndrome would remain with me well into my adulthood.) I remembered being afraid to ask a girl, any girl, to the prom. I remembered turning down the opportunity one summer to join an ensemble magic show touring the eastern United States and Canada because I was afraid to leave home. I remembered my senior year in high school, when I first discovered that alcohol could put my fear to sleep for a while.

I remembered all of this in an instant, as if it was downloaded into my mind with the fastest technology available. I thought, "This must be what people describing near-death experiences call the life review." I remembered the fear of my entire adult life, and my constant attempts to put the fear out with alcohol, like water on a fire. I remembered my best intentions to write books, to be a good boyfriend, and later a good husband all being contaminated by fear. I recognized how I had disguised my fear with anger and cynicism, and how my best efforts had gone toward denying and running from the fear.

I don't include my personal experiences in this book because I have faced and overcome insurmountable odds. You will see that many of my clients' stories are far more powerful than mine in this regard. I see my story more as an example of the typical, middle-of-the-road, Western-world neurotic experience with fear. I have been speaking to audiences for years and have never found a group of people who do not identify with at least some of my struggle with fear and all of its various associations with self-doubt, anger, and perfectionism.

I believe that fear has become a bad habit for most of us. Maybe it is a side effect of our techno-efficient world. In other words, maybe we have too much time on our hands.

Several years ago, shortly after my wife and I had moved to our farm just outside of Nashville, an uncharacteristically severe ice storm descended upon us, leaving us without electricity, phone service, and passable roadways for about a week. Our menagerie consists of the usual dogs and cats, with chickens, ducks, goats, and horses thrown in for good measure. Basically I married the real-world version of Ellie Mae Clampett—meaning, I married into a life populated with lots of critters. That week we all spent together on our new farm without any real access to the rest of the world proved very educational.

We awoke in front of the fireplace, where we slept for very good reason (the average temperature that week was around 9 degrees Fahrenheit), built the fire back up, and then began our morning chores of feeding all the animals and breaking the thick ice that constantly formed in the water troughs. Since our house is on a hill with a steep driveway between the house and the main barn, plenty of walking—more like slipping and sliding—up and down the hill was included in our daily chores. The world was one big sheet of ice to us for that one week.

We did the morning work, returned to the fire to regain feeling in our hands and feet, rested awhile, then ate lunch. In the early afternoon, we had more chores—breaking the ice in the water troughs was never ending—but we also had a little time to talk and play before it was time to feed everyone again. We wanted to have everything done before dark, because it was just easier in the light of day, but also because when the sun was gone, it was colder.

When the sun was gone and our fire restoked, we gathered the dogs and invited the cats to join us in our nest of blankets and pillows in front of the fireplace. Dakota, our golden retriever, was especially popular because he was so warm. We only had two dogs at the time, but those were definitely "three-dog nights."

My wife, Dede, and I talked for a while some nights or read by candlelight or flashlight, but mostly we were tired and cold and it was dark, so we slept. The next morning we started all over again.

A couple of months after the ice finally melted, as I was

talking about the experience with a friend, I realized that for that one week, sentenced by Mother Nature to manual labor at below-freezing temperatures, I had not experienced any of the low-level, constant anxiety I had become accustomed to in my daily life. I know I complained about the inconvenience and the discomfort, but I had spent an entire week without worrying. Except for my great hopes for the return of electricity (I never missed the telephone much) to our lives, I had not spent my days mentally projecting into the future or fretting about to-do lists, the phone calls I needed to make, or the clients I was scheduled to see . . . tomorrow.

Unlike the trip to my alma mater that catapulted me into the past, the ice storm of those many years ago had planted me firmly in the present. It had been quite literally a Zen-like "chop wood, carry water" experience. And since that time I have realized that, to a significant degree, the depressions and the anxieties so many of us accept as a natural part of our daily lives are anything but natural. (One important aspect to be noted here is that Dede and I not only had spent a week focused in the present moment, but also were—probably for the first time in our adult lives—not sleep deprived.) When I was challenged to get up in the morning because wood had to be put on the fire and Dede, the critters, and I had to eat and drink, the only problems I had were the present-moment ones that I confronted and solved one at a time. The Bully was absent, and the Ally did his best work, guiding me from one necessary task to the next.

Frequently I will make the point with a client, as we sit in my well-lit and air-conditioned office, that to the degree that we can successfully bring ourselves into the present moment, experiencing only the chairs in which we are seated and the company we are keeping, neither of us will have a problem. Either of us could easily and quickly travel backward in time for some regret or guilt or forward for some version of fear, but in this moment there is no problem. This is just as true for you as you read this sentence. With the exception of a potential present-tense physiologically based affliction (i.e., physical pain, or emotional distress caused by faulty brain chemistry), you will have to travel outside of this moment to find a problem.

My intention is not to oversimplify the potential solution to our battles with fear, but to make an important point: *the great majority of the emotional distress we experience results from how we think about ourselves and our circumstances, rather than the circumstances themselves.*

The Student Union Building was one of the older structures on the campus. As I approached, only I could see the hundreds of memories that filled it. To the present-day students, it was business as usual, and I was just some unremarkable older guy wandering through.

The little voice seemed bigger now, more like a presence. The feeling was not unprecedented; since before my Austin College days I have sensed that something or someone worked with me, specifically in regard to my writing. I know that can sound a little strange. Before you close the book with an "Oh, right, now he's going to tell me he's a channeler," please understand that I am not sure what or who it is. Through the years, I have believed and not believed many things about the experience. What I find undeniable is that there is something associated with me that is wiser than I am. Or maybe it's a place deep within my consciousness where I keep wisdom that is not normally available to me. Regardless, I can say beyond all doubt that I have benefited 100 percent of the times I have felt its presence. A conversation with God? A spirit guide? A dead relative with nothing better to do? Or just a wiser part of my own crowded mind? I'm pretty sure the answer doesn't matter, as long as I remain willing to listen to what it has to say.

Whatever or whoever the source of the voice (it's more like receiving complete packages of thoughts than it is like actually hearing a voice; it's not a very auditory experience), it was definitely with me that night on my campus stroll.

"Thom, you are still scared," it said. "Fear still has too much power in your life."

This experience was not simple self-criticism; it was a reality check felt through my whole being. I knew my life had been more than just fear. I did not forget the obstacles I had overcome or the courage that had guided me into and through some of the darkest places in my consciousness. I had been in recovery from alcoholism for a dozen years and been successfully treated for depression for six years. I had a well-established therapy practice in which I guided many others through difficult times, important discoveries, and life-changing decisions. I had written and published several books, accomplishing a lifelong dream. But the fear was always there. My first marriage had not survived, but now I was happily married, living in a real-life, healthy, adult relationship. But the fear was always there. It had always been there.

In spite of all I had accomplished and all I was grateful for, I realized in that moment not only that fear had always been there, but also that much of the time fear was still in charge. Although in many ways I was different from the young man who had graduated from Austin College twenty-five years before, I still had something very much in common with him.

As I walked from one end of that campus and back, I was in class once again. Forget about the lecture I was there to give; here is the lecture I was apparently there to get. Even though I cannot explain exactly how it works, these are the words I heard, or felt, or both:

"Pay close attention. Listen carefully. Let's look at what happens when fear is in charge.

"With fear in charge, you can never fully relax, let your guard down, be your true self. You can't open up because you are afraid of how people will respond if they were to meet the real you. When fear is in charge, you simply cannot take that chance. Fear will not allow honesty, fear despises spontaneity, and fear refuses to believe in you. Fear may mean well, but it ruins everything by overprotecting you, insisting that you stay hidden and keep a low profile, promising that your time is coming . . . sometime later.

"Fear is bold, but insists that you be timid. Take a

chance and there will be hell to pay: fear will call on its dear friend, shame, to meet you on the other side of your risk taking, to tell you what you should not have done. Fear will trip you, tackle you, smother you, do whatever it takes to cause you to hesitate, to stop you. In this way fear is fearless.

"Fear will remain in charge for as long as you let it. It will never volunteer to step down, to relinquish its authority.

"Your assignment is to live a life that is not ruled by fear. To do this, you must be able to identify, at any given time, exactly what fear is telling you—or rather threatening you with—and to disobey its instructions. Every morning when you awake, make a conscious decision to remain in charge of your own life. Fear cannot occupy the space in which you stand. Fear cannot force you out of that position of authority, but it can, if you let it, scare you away.

"Let your personal motto be 'NO FEAR.' Say those two powerful words as you put your feet on the floor, as you look into the mirror, as you walk out the door. Ask yourself each morning, and all through the day, what will NO FEAR mean for me today?

"Ask yourself the question . . . and don't forget to listen for the answer."

I wrote that lecture down when I returned to my hotel room and thought about the answer to that question. What does the NO FEAR motto mean to me? I realized that NO FEAR means that I will not let fear determine my every move. It means that I will look the Bully straight in the eye and say, "No, you cannot control my life. I am in charge here." And I realized that NO FEAR does not mean that there will be "no fear," but that I am committing to saying NO to fear. And then I realized that I had just been firmly, but lovingly, shoved off my safe little ledge into my next free fall. The evening walk would serve as the catalyst for a brand-new growth spurt.

I write to you now from somewhere inside that growth spurt. I have taken the lecture to heart—and mind. (The Nutshell reads: "Heart and mind work best as equal partners.") I have done my best, as the imperfect human that I am, to carry the NO FEAR motto with me every day. What seems just as important is the time I have spent reflecting on fear as the great common denominator that it is. The present-tense practice of the NO FEAR motto has helped me take important new steps in both the personal and professional aspects of my life, but it has also given me new lenses through which to view our human condition. The ideas and the stories in this book are my report to you from my perspective with the new lenses.

I hope you will try on these lenses too. I encourage you to adopt the NO FEAR motto as your own. Find ways to bring it to mind throughout the day. One of my clients, Lynn, keeps the words "NO FEAR" taped to her bathroom mirror, and the initials, "N.F." on her refrigerator and on the steering wheel of her car. "The initials remind me of the NO FEAR motto," Lynn told me, "without anyone else knowing what they represent." When Lynn starts her computer at work, the letters "N.F." even appear on her screen.

The more you rehearse the NO FEAR motto, the more natural it will become. Don't think that the motto will replace or take away fear, because it won't. Just install the NO FEAR motto right next to your fear. Remember that the little voice told me that "the assignment is to live a life that is not ruled by fear." It didn't say anything about being without fear.

Repeat the motto to yourself frequently throughout the day. Make it your mantra. Whether this feels like a powerful spiritual practice or simply something to mutter under your breath, make it a habit. Before you begin something that feels stressful to you—giving a speech, talking to the boss, standing up to a friend or family member—close your eyes for just one moment, take a few deep breaths, and repeat the motto slowly with each breath.

When you adopt the NO FEAR motto, you are making a commitment to the first letter of our acronym map: *facing fear.* Ironically, the only way to activate the NO FEAR motto in your life is to move directly toward the fear. Don't expect to fully comprehend this all at once anymore than you would expect to simply exorcise all fear from your life. It is progress we seek, not perfection.

I, like you, am a work in progress. As a clinician, teacher, writer, and human being, I claim to be no more than that. In fact, the self-help gurus who write and teach from a position of "Once upon a time, when I was as screwed up as you are" have always gotten on my nerves. Actually, anyone who denies the essential subjectivity of individual experience by claiming to have "the" answer for all of us, gets on my nerves.

Long ago I gave up on the idea of completion when it comes to personal growth. One of the Nutshells reads: "All things in turmoil in and around you are evidence that you are still alive." There will always be more to do, more to learn, and, as we will explore in a later chapter, each of us has certain themes that will recur in the progression of our life lessons. Fear is frequently—if not always—at the center of these lessons. And by learning to transform our relationship to fear, we set off a powerful ripple effect that just might change everything.

My goal, which certainly includes sharing my personal experience and my work helping others, is ultimately to inspire you to think and feel and explore for yourself. We all have little voices speaking to us. And if I can assist your little voice in moving you into your next growth spurt, I will have a success on my hands.

On the morning after, the day I was scheduled to give my own lecture, I put on my brand-new "NO FEAR" motto even before I put on my eyeglasses, before I brushed my teeth. I delivered my speech to a mixed crowd of students and faculty. I saw some old friends from my college days, who remarked on how much I had changed since then—they were referring to my lecture on self-compassion and personal responsibility, not my waistline and hair color. What they didn't know was how much I was only just beginning to change, thanks to my new personal motto: NO FEAR.

Later that day I was joking with one of my psychology professors about a recurring dream I had had ever since leaving college. In the dream I am distressed because I have forgotten to check my campus post-office box. There is something there I need to get, but I cannot because I am no longer enrolled in school. It occurs to me only now, as I write this, that my recurring dream has likely found its resolution; I have not had the dream again. There was in fact something—an important message—I had left behind when I graduated. One evening twenty-five years later, I returned to listen to one final lecture and pick up a message I believe was intended for me all along: NO FEAR.

The following day, flying back to Nashville, I thought about the lecture. "Let's look at what happens when fear is in charge," it began. I thought about my life, and I thought about the work I do with others. What occurred to me seemed too simple, offensively simple. But each time I approached it, like trying to get 2 + 2 to equal something other than 4, I came up with the same answer: how we relate to fear determines how we do in life, and maybe it is the essence of who we are.

CHAPTER THREE

Walking Kirby to Class
Facing Big Fear

To conquer fear is the beginning of wisdom.
—BERTRAND RUSSELL

WHEN MY GODSON, WYNN, was six years old, he was very aware that his daddy went to work every day and that his daddy was a lawyer. He wanted to know what I did every day. Where did I go to work? What did I do?

I explained my workday as a psychotherapist in what I thought was my best six-year-old language and, like a veteran shrink himself, Wynn responded with a clear and accurate paraphrase. "People come to visit you," he summarized.

"Yes," I said, "that is exactly right."

What a great job I have! People come to visit me. I have conversations for a living—interesting and meaningful conversations. And for this I get paid.

As I reflect on my interesting career choice, I can see that another way to describe what I do is this: I stand with people as they face their fears. I help them lift their heads and look directly and carefully at the walls of resistance engineered and constructed by fear. I help them, when they are ready, to speak the words "No Fear." I help them place their palms firmly on those walls, and I help them push. Many people along the way—friends, teachers, colleagues, and my own therapists—have helped me to do the same. For this, I am eternally grateful.

Over the past twenty years, I have accompanied men and women as they faced fears of all sizes—small, medium, and large. The life circumstances associated with the fears come in many forms as well, from the young man who came to see me to bolster his confidence after receiving a significant promotion at work, to clients who have endured terrible abuse as children, to those who face tremendous losses as adults.

Many, if not most, express some judgment of themselves, something to the effect that their problems are not as important as others'. Although it is true that battling a persistent case of Sunday night anxiety or Monday morning depression is a less severe problem than posttraumatic stress disorder stemming from childhood sexual abuse, the consequences are just as real.

Here is something else to consider when you find yourself comparing your problems with others': a fear manifesting as a low-intensity but chronic anxiety is probably only the tip of the iceberg. With exploration, that Sunday anxiety or Monday depression usually leads to deeper fears about who you are, what you are doing with your life, and even the ultimate meaning of life. If you judge yourself too quickly, you may interfere with an opportunity to discover those bigger fears beneath the consistent worry for which you have built a tolerance. Using our acronym map, once we are *facing* a fear, the next important step is to *explore* it. It is part of my job to be sure we dive beneath the surface, so we can genuinely heal from the inside out, rather than slap one more Band-Aid on a broken leg. One of the Nutshells on my wall reminds us: "Growth always moves from the inside out."

I use a simple technique to help people quickly discover their bigger fears. It's a real time-saver. I call it "climbing down the ladder"; as you will see, a simple succession of sentence completions forms the rungs to the ladder. Here is how it works.

I asked Matthew, who was expressing his fear about pursuing a change of careers, "What are you afraid of?"

Matthew answered, "I'm afraid of failing, especially since I would be giving up a successful and stable career to do this."

I bring out the ladder so Matthew can climb down and discover more about his fear. "I want you to respond with the first thoughts that come to your mind: If I change careers and fail, then . . . "

". . . I will feel terrible," Matthew says.

I guide him to the next rung: "If I fail and feel terrible . . . "

". . . my wife will never forgive me."

"If my wife never forgives me . . . "

". . . I will lose her."

"If I lose my wife . . . "

". . . I'll be alone." Matthew's shoulders drop, his eyes are downcast; he is feeling his "aloneness." His defeated body language tells me that this is a big one.

I continue. "If I am alone . . . "

Matthew pauses. I can almost see the emotion beginning to fill him. He speaks more slowly. "If I am alone . . ." his shoulders drop even more, "I am nothing."

I decide to take him down one more rung. "If I am nothing . . . "

". . . my whole life will be wasted."

Using the "ladder," Matthew and I can continue and no doubt discover even more about his fear, but at this point we have plenty to work with.

Matthew is forty-five years old, a successful human resource director for a fairly large company who was thinking about opening his own consulting and training business, specializing in conflict resolution. He is a thorough, even a little compulsive, man who has already done his homework—including lining up potential customers for his new business—regarding this career move. There is of course natural fear about making the change, but the fear that is getting in his way is the neurotic fear, the Bully.

Matthew is becoming paralyzed not by the understandable fear that his new business could fail, but by the much louder, much stronger fears that his new business will fail, that his wife will then leave him, that he will be alone, and that his entire life will have been wasted. Now those are some big fears. Can you distinguish the Ally from the Bully in this situation?

If we had not used the "ladder," Matthew and I might have wasted some time, and some of his money, talking about his resistance to the change as if it were based in his fear that the business might fail. By using the "ladder" we put the first two letters of our acronym map into play: *face* it, *explore* it.

Sometime when you are feeling stuck or confused, ask yourself, "What am I afraid of?" Listen for the first answer that occurs to you, and then climb down your own ladder. Don't run from the fear; turn to face it; go looking for the most powerful, threatening part of the fear by climbing down your ladder. The chances of solving a problem are greatly enhanced by accurately defining the problem. Fear of a failed business and fear of an entire life wasted are two very different problems. With the accurate information—the truth about Matthew's fear—Matthew and I were able to use the next two letters in our acronym map to free him to make decisions based on his business intelligence and his true desires.

Matthew further explored his deep fears of being alone and wasting his life. By realizing that these fears originated in some childhood experiences, he was able to *accept* that his Bully was threatening him with outdated fears, and he was able to *respond* to the Bully's neurotic fear by disagreeing with the premise that even in a worst-case scenario—a failed business—he would not have to be alone and his life would not be wasted. Matthew was able to proceed with the creation of his new business, fully aware that his Bully would be attempting to sabotage his efforts by threatening Matthew with some of his worst fears.

When you identify and keep moving toward neurotic fears, you accomplish two things. First, you minimize the chances of a successful surprise attack from the Bully, since you are keeping the light of awareness shining on his scowling face. And, second, you reduce the Bully's credibility when you step forward, look him squarely in the eye, and say, "Okay, you have my full attention. Tell me again about all the bad stuff that is going to happen to me if I don't listen to you. Be sure to make it sound real scary."

When I am paying attention, as my little voice tells me to do, every single person with whom I work has something to teach me. Matthew's story is a good example of knowing when the best strategy is to look straight through our fears, challenge their credibility, and allow our diminishing belief in them to destroy their power over us. At other times, the fear encountered is not an empty threat, but is instead completely legitimate. This was never more true than the two years I spent learning valuable lessons about life, and about death, with a remarkable woman named Kirby.

Out here, in the so-called real world, to the untrained eye I was a psychotherapist and Kirby was my client. I was the shop owner and she was the customer. And in all the official, appropriate ways, it remained so—from beginning to end.

In the real real world, the grayer territory located much closer to the truth, our roles were not so easily defined. Sometimes Kirby was the therapist and I was the client. Sometimes I was the student, sometimes she was. But most of the time Kirby and I were classmates, lab partners. Her cancer was the real teacher.

There were times when it felt as though I was the one facing death, and in a way I was—admittedly from a much safer distance than Kirby. She was trying to make up her mind; it was a "to be or not to be" kind of thing. I guess that was one of the many trades we made along the way. I helped her to have an open and honest debate with herself, and she taught me how to die. More specifically, she taught me that when my time comes, I just might pull it off with a little dignity.

Several months after the initial cancer diagnosis, Kirby and I discovered that she was quite literally of two minds on the subject of her life. We investigated with a simple gestalt therapy technique: Kirby moved from one chair to the other, playing out both parts of the conversation that had—again, literally—become a matter of life and death for her.

One part of Kirby wanted her to live. This part took her to the doctor and drove her to one kind of therapy or another. This part meditated, prayed, and became a walking encyclopedia of information about cancer and cancer treatments. This part spoke about a deep desire to break free from the old, outdated beliefs she had absorbed from her family as a child. Kirby had already made undeniable progress in separating from the rigid and negative thinking of her parents. She lived an enlightened life, really. She taught meditation classes. She had explored many interesting avenues of spiritual and metaphysical practice. She was certainly an informed and open-minded woman, and in this way 180 degrees from her mother. This part, the one that wanted Kirby to live, was more confused than discouraged by the persistent cancer. "Why would such an enormous obstacle show up just as I am finally ready to live like I've never lived before?" she asked me one day.

"I have no idea," was my reply. How's that for sage wisdom?

The other part of Kirby, the part we identified in the other chair of the exercise, wanted Kirby to die. Or that was what we thought at first. As is often the case with this simple two-chair exercise, when Kirby sat in this chair, she thought quite differently from the Kirby I had come to know. Again, as is often the case with this exercise, even the tone and cadence of her voice were different.

This part provided a very different point of view, but it wasn't some sort of anti-Kirby. It wasn't Kirby's opposite; it was just different. This part did not ascribe to the misguided, negative beliefs of her family either. This part was just tired and wanted Kirby to give up—to rest. This part could acknowledge the progress, but it wasn't enough. It was always pointing out how far there was yet to go, and that in spite of all the progress life was still very difficult. (Kirby had struggled for years with depression, and almost total dissatisfaction when it came to her desire for a primary relationship.)

Kirby described this part as a "constant pain in the butt," and she found it very interesting that her cancer had originally shown up as a chronic, intense pain in her lower back. I thought of this part as a brilliant attorney with an endless supply of evidence to support its argument—specifically seeking a death sentence. In short, this part of Kirby could really bring a party to a screeching halt. That is why Kirby named this part "Party Pooper."

Some days we just talked, going wherever the conversation would take us. Other days, Kirby would faithfully move from one chair to the other, inviting the conversation within her to play out. Then one day (I don't even remember who caught on first), we got it. The lightbulb switched on above both of our heads. We had been missing a very significant point: both parts of Kirby wanted to live. Yes, essentially they wanted the exact same thing. The problem was not one of life or death. The problem was that there existed in Kirby's consciousness two completely different definitions of life.

That was a very productive day in class.

Kirby felt a new hope with our discovery. "After all," Kirby said, "they say that accurately defining the problem is three-fourths of the solution, right?"

"Right," I answered, certain that somebody must have said that somewhere, sometime. If not, we had said it now. And we believed it.

You see, the part of Kirby that so effectively represented death as the only good option was actually very spiritually oriented. This so-called Party Pooper not only did not fear death, but literally did not believe in death. Ironically, this part had developed from Kirby's years of meditation training and spiritual exploration. This part *knew* that what we called death was merely transition. And this part, exhausted by the human experience and dreading the prospect of continuing, was ready to get on with what it considered "life without the limits, restrictions, and burdens of physical existence."

I think of Kirby's internal disagreement about the definition of life whenever I work with clients who seem to be more afraid of life than they are of death. These are the people who will not be particularly motivated if someone were to tell them that their alcoholism, their depression, or their eating disorder just might kill them. It is important to remember that death is sometimes not only a lousy deterrent, but that it can be a powerful motivator, consciously or unconsciously. My work with Kirby taught me to keep asking questions when we arrive at the desire for (or apathy toward) death.

With our new insight, Kirby and I celebrated our brilliance. We were certain now that we could beat the cancer. I am no stranger to studies and testimonials of mind over matter, but Kirby was a die-hard believer (no pun intended). Her depth of belief was contagious, and it felt great. We were the winning team, the underdogs destined to come from behind to win the game. My preference for sports analogies was not as contagious; Kirby maintained a less competitive view of our work—most of the time.

We both struggled off and on with the question of whether to love the cancer into remission (we were both children of the 1960s, after all) or to stand firm and beat it senseless. One of my favorite and lasting memories is a guided visualization session in which Kirby introduced the character she called "Terminator Mama."

We laughed hard at the image of Terminator Mama—a powerful woman with armor and weapons—but by that time I was praying that she was as tough as she sounded. Kirby was weakening. She didn't want to talk about it yet, maybe she was still trying to deny it, but it was becoming more and more obvious.

At the time I thought of what was happening as failure. I wasn't making the grade, and as a result my lab partner was going to die. Within my own consciousness, fear and guilt were getting a lot of airtime.

With benefit of hindsight, I think Kirby and I had (for God knows what reason) been bumped up to a more advanced class, to learn a lesson that neither of us had the slightest interest in learning.

There was always the pain. Kirby described it as an intense burning from deep inside her, but she didn't talk about it much. I'm pretty sure the discouragement hurt her worse.

It had become impractical, and often impossible, for Kirby to get to my office. Sometime shortly before the advent of Terminator Mama we began meeting in Kirby's apartment. We usually met for an hour to an hour and a half, depending on how she was feeling. I remember one session in which it took Kirby ten or fifteen minutes to make it from her bedroom to the living room (forty-five feet at most), where we had our meetings. The hospice nurse was there; she and I tried to talk Kirby into having the meeting in her bedroom. Kirby would have no part of it. Straining with every step, leaning on her walker as heavily as she could with her weakened arms, she finally made it to the living room, where she literally collapsed onto the sofa, gasping for breath as if she had just run a marathon. Beyond making sure she landed on the sofa and not the floor as she let herself drop forward, there was nothing I could do. Nothing except watch Kirby's pain, and the courage that came with it.

From the sofa, she smiled just slightly. "I need to rest a minute or so," she said, still out of breath. I touched her face and hair and did the talking that afternoon. Kirby closed her eyes and rested.

Throughout our visualization sessions, Kirby would make every effort to see herself as a vibrant, healthy adult attending to the beautiful child within her. Inevitably, the strong adult would slip away or not appear at all. Kirby would be the child, vulnerable and in desperate need of parental protection and love. We never left the child alone, of course. Kirby had selected very specific images of "Spirit Parents," with whom we would always leave Little Kirby at the end of a visualization session. We both came to believe in those Spirit Parents, and we believed that no matter what happened, Kirby would survive. Remember, she and I had already learned that there is more than one way to define life.

We exchanged gifts. We had given each other books along the way, but this was different, very important to us both. I found myself challenged by the awareness that any material gift for Kirby would be no gift at all. I was just completing work on an audiotape project about self-compassion (*Practice Makes Practice*); I didn't have the actual tape yet, so I brought the script to her and told her that I was dedicating the project to her. The dedication reads:

To Kirby, with love, gratitude, and respect.
Your courage is my teacher.

Kirby was lying on her side in her bed, in a sort of half-fetal position, not strong enough to hold the seventy-five-page script for more than a few seconds. She directed me to her dresser, to the bottom left drawer, to two beautiful, perfectly round crystal balls—one about the size of a pool ball, the other the size of a golf ball. Kirby told me she had given this a lot of thought and decided she wanted me to have these two crystals, objects that she associated not only with life, but specifically with life on earth.

School was coming to a close, and I was going to miss my classmate, my lab partner, my student, and my teacher.

Two days after we exchanged our gifts, I got a call from one of Kirby's friends, saying that she had taken a turn for the worse, that her doctor had been to the apartment and had brought plenty of morphine to help Kirby with the pain. The friend told me Kirby was asleep a lot of the time now, but was still awake and talking for short periods. I made arrangements to visit the next day.

Kirby was awake when I arrived. It was early evening, six-thirty or seven. I remember it was just getting dark outside. She was in a hospital bed. A hospice nurse was at the apartment, as were a couple of Kirby's friends. We had our last session that night.

I sat close, so I could touch her face and hair. That had become our way of connecting when she didn't feel like talking. I asked how she was feeling, and she said "Bad," smiling a little, as much as she could, I think. I suggested she close her eyes and relax as much as was possible. I asked if she could see herself as a completely healthy adult, fully physically restored, and without hesitation she said yes. I asked if she could see her child-self, the one we had worked so hard to care for over the past months, and again she said yes. I suggested that the healthy, very alive adult go to the child, and she did.

The physically healthy, fully restored Kirby took the child into her arms, held her very close, and smiled. A great big smile. The little girl snuggled her face into Kirby's neck and breathed a giant sigh of relief.

The Kirby on the hospital bed smiled too, just slightly more than before—again, as much as she could. Kirby's breathing eased a little; she seemed to be asleep. I kissed her cheek and said good-bye.

I have had, and will continue to have, other role models for living with courage, but I cannot imagine anyone having a more powerful impact than Kirby. She taught me many things, including this: "Courage is to fear as light is to darkness." You guessed it—that sentence is right in the middle of my wall of Nutshells.

I keep a book she gave me during her last round of chemotherapy on my writing desk at home. Just to hold the book reminds me there is nothing that I cannot face with

courage and dignity. I hope I bring that message to others—
to everyone my life touches, in fact. I hope there is something of that wisdom in what I have to teach Matthew and
the other people you will read about in this book, and to you
who read it. The book Kirby gave me is open on my desk
right now. The inscription reads:

To Thom with deepest love.
Thanks for helping me find the joy within.
From my child to your child "Namaste"—

KIRBY 8–'91

Before Kirby and I had our little adventure, I was certain
I would embarrass myself whenever it was my turn to show
up at death's door. "What a wimp," one of the Spirit Guide
Evaluation Committee (S.G.E.C.) would say, shaking her
head slowly in disgust.

"A complete cry baby," my designated spirit guide would
add in agreement, more than a little embarrassed himself.

Several months before Kirby died, that changed. I couldn't
identify the exact time, but I could take you to the exact
place in Kirby's living room where I was sitting when I knew.
"I can do this," I thought. That's all there was to it. You
might say for such a significant, even life-changing, revela-
tion it was rather understated, anticlimactic really. But it
didn't matter. The job was done, that particular lesson
learned. This is not to say I have lost all fear of death—no
way. But in that moment I knew when my time comes, when
I do show up at death's door, I will have what it takes to ring

the bell and stand there with my self-respect intact. Kirby showed me how it's done. She was my role model.

Role models come in all sizes and shapes and colors, and in all circumstances. Kirby demonstrated courage as she fought for life and as she faced death. A teacher in a small town might be the most important role model in the life of a young person who grows up to become a world leader, who, in turn, becomes a role model for children in a thousand small towns. An alcoholic parent, providing a negative example in personal relationships, might be a positive role model as someone who values creativity. Everyone is eligible; perfection is not a requirement.

On September 11, 2001, the world witnessed the actions of thousands of positive role models—the firefighters, police officers, emergency personnel, and citizens who responded to the terrorist attacks on the World Trade Center in New York City and the Pentagon in Washington, D.C. Then we heard the story of the airline passengers who foiled the efforts of the terrorists who had hijacked a fourth plane, also intended for Washington, D.C. We were all left asking ourselves, "Would I respond with the same courage in the face of my worst nightmare?" That is what role models do: inspire us to ask such questions. By their example they challenge us to consider where we stand in relation to our fears.

Who are your role models? Who did you look up to in childhood? Who are your role models today? You can never have too many. Kirby is just one of mine.

Namaste, Kirby.

CHAPTER FOUR

Making a Run for It
Getting to Fear

When you get beyond fear, you feel free.
—Spencer Johnson, M.D.

The clients I saw during the weeks that followed the horrific events of September 11, 2001, expressed a myriad of responses, including shock, fear, and deep sadness. But we all had one response in common: we saw our day-to-day concerns and problems from a new perspective. What was a big deal one moment was barely a blip on our emotional radar screens the next.

As the shock wore off, and as we all began to deal with the feelings below the shock, many of us experienced a strange guilty feeling. As we settled back into our daily routines, we felt guilty when we began to think that those little blips on the emotional radar screen were big deals again.

"It's not realistic to expect yourself to no longer have personal problems," I told one client who had expressed a great deal of guilt about having any feeling other than compassion for the victims of the terrorist attacks.

"But everything I bring up seems so insignificant now," she said.

"Part of that response is good for all of us," I told her. "It will be great if we can do a better job now of keeping things in perspective, of realizing when something doesn't need to be a big deal." In other words, I was telling her that it will be great if we can pay less attention to the Bully and more attention to the Ally.

"But paying attention to our dissatisfactions, even our little complaints, can also have a positive effect," I continued, "especially if we realize that often they are trying to communicate something deeper than the surface complaint. It's all about listening to ourselves."

It is true we humans are a complaining lot, myself included. We have—and make excellent use of—the capacity to complain about almost everything. We complain about the cold in February and the heat in July. We close a deal on a new house, then complain about what a hassle moving is. We love someone who is relaxed and laid back, then complain when he is ten minutes late for our lunch date. We enjoy our lunch, and complain about the crowded restaurant. We love our job, but complain about the work. It's sort of like joining the gym to lift weights, then complaining about how heavy they are.

When compared to "real problems," everyday complaints do seem petty. You would think that experiences like the one I had with Kirby, and especially the events of September 11, 2001, would severely disable our ability to complain about the little things. Not really. That is not to say the lessons learned are lost, but it would be less than honest to say that we do not have a tendency fall back to sleep.

Another Nutshell on my wall reads: "The human condition is one of chronic forgetfulness." We become enlightened through our experiences with one another; then the light fades. This characteristic forgetfulness is simultaneously the bad news and the good news. The bad news is how easily we forget, how quickly we can misplace the wisdom we had just a moment ago. The good news is that we need each other to be reminded. I think of it as God's way of reminding us to stay in touch.

Left to our own imperfect, very leaky, human memory, it works like getting a speeding ticket. After getting the ticket, we drive within the speed limit—especially along the stretch of road where we were caught—but with time (surprisingly little time), the foot becomes heavier and we are once again happily exceeding the speed limit, no longer thinking of the potential consequences.

Between tickets, maybe even instead of tickets, we could remind each other to slow down. If we do that, chronic human forgetfulness becomes an asset, motivating us to remain connected to each other. I can offer some terrific advice to a client or friend today, and within twenty-four hours need someone to give me the exact same advice. For this to happen, however, we must remain in touch with one another. How else can we send and receive distress calls?

One of the ways we send out distress calls, demonstrating our need to be reminded, is complaining. It is far from the cleanest communication, certainly not the most effective, but listening to our complaints with a willingness to climb down the ladder is at least a starting point. Rather than discount our human tendency to complain, I try to make good use of it. A complaint that seems petty or meaningless is just at the top of the ladder. By bitching and moaning about this and that, we avoid taking the ladder down to discover the bigger fears below. So instead of simply criticizing ourselves for complaining (which is essentially complaining about our complaining), it serves us well to look more closely at the nature of our complaints.

Sure, some of us complain more than others. The ability to complain is definitely not evenly distributed among us. And we complain in a variety of ways. Some of us are moaners and groaners, some are whiners, some of us are excellent pouters, and others are martyrs who pretend to never complain. Still others don't seem like complainers at all. They are characterized more by their shame and self-loathing. These are complainers too; they are just complaining about themselves.

Let's define the term more specifically. I think of a complainer as a dissatisfied person who is not thinking like a problem solver. My thesaurus tells me a complainer is "a malcontent, a lamenter, a fault-finder" who is investing more energy in the expression of displeasure than in responding to, and solving, the problem. Remember the Serenity Prayer?

God, grant me the serenity
to accept the things I cannot change,
the courage to change the things I can,
and the wisdom to know the difference.

Complainers apply it backward, putting lots of energy into what they cannot possibly change, and ignoring the often simple but powerful aspects of a situation in which they could effect significant change.

Working with clients as a psychotherapist, with groups in seminars, and with audiences as a speaker, I sometimes think of myself as an energy-efficiency consultant. I help people discover their energy leaks: the ways they are thinking and behaving that drain them of the vitality needed to solve their problems. Through years in this business, listening and collaborating with hundreds of clients for thousands of hours, facilitating scores of personal-growth workshops, and being the proud recipient of plenty of psychotherapy myself, I have arrived at an awareness that is neither original nor surprising. Listen to the complaints, identify the energy leaks, put your ear to door of your consciousness, and there you will discover something we all have in common: fear.

Having been in this business long enough now to get the lay of the land, I am more frequently invited to speak to professional groups—other psychotherapists, counselors, social workers, and so on. When given these opportunities I always talk with my colleagues about how important it is to see our work with clients as a collaborative effort. My wife, a professional counselor, tells her clients she wants to work "with them," not "on them." I believe that approach can make all the difference in the effectiveness of psychotherapy.

If I am to be a worthy collaborator in this work of confronting the fears that underlie our complaints, then I had better make certain I am willing to do the same work I am asking my clients, seminar participants, audiences, and readers to do.

I recently told a group of about fifty of my fellow head-shrinkers: "If I want to learn to play the guitar, I will find a teacher who is proficient in playing the guitar. If I travel to Africa to go on safari, I will seek a guide with experience. I am not the least bit interested in a guitar teacher who doesn't know how to play guitar or a safari guide who has studied the maps, but has never been in the jungle. In the same way, if we expect our clients to trust us to help them do their work, we had better be sure we have done—and continue to do—our own."

I also gave each of my fellow shrinks a copy of the Nutshell that says: "The difference between knowledge and wisdom is experience."

If you choose to shop for a therapist, be sure to ask the candidates what kind of personal-growth work they have done, what kind of therapy they have been in. If you run across those who are noticeably uncomfortable with your question, or if they respond with some vague, reflective comment about how it seems important for you to take the focus off of yourself, stand up, say adios, and get the hell out of there. Keep moving until you find someone who will look you in the eye and tell you something real about themselves.

With or without a therapist, one of the most difficult challenges we face when we decide to roll up our sleeves and move toward our fears is the challenge of gathering both cognitive and emotional information about ourselves and then resisting the temptation to immediately "do something" with what we are discovering. Certainly the goal of any personal-growth work is change, but when we move too quickly to take action, we are more likely acting from well-rehearsed patterns of psychological defense than we are acting from a place of readiness and courage. The tendency is to react rather than act; a defensive reflex takes us out of discomfort before we have a chance to learn from it. Remember that *exploration* and *acceptance* precede *responding* in our acronym map.

Our tendency to jump the gun and immediately move to an active response is testament to our desire to be "in control" of our lives. When we value "being in control," above all else—essentially expecting the impossible—we are actually giving the Bully control. The Bully tells us that if we can just keep everything aligned and in order (ducks in a row), we won't have problems, pain, or stress. Promising us this impossible dream, the Bully scares us about the very essence of our humanness, otherwise known as imperfection. It is vital that we accept our normal limitations. I have worked with perfectionists who believed that their challenge was to accept that they will never quite reach perfection. I am quick to point out how unrealistic that is. We don't fall a little short of perfection. We are human; we can't even see perfection from where we are standing. The Nutshell reads: "To be addicted to control is to be endlessly out of control."

When my wife and I were stranded on our farm for a week during the ice storm, we did not experience the Bully's harassment about perfection—that low-level, constant anxiety telling us that we must be in control at all times. Our circumstances made clear that we did not control a lot, and the things we could control demanded our attention. We built and maintained the fire, broke ice in the water troughs, and fed ourselves and our animals. We got plenty of rest, and then we started our chores over again. The Bully was absent. Maybe he went to a nice warm hotel. But The Ally guided us to the tasks that required action. Basic survival. He did not overreact, demanding that we immediately do this or that or telling us we should have done this or that yesterday. Instead, the Ally calmly provided us with clear, concise advice and direction. His philosophy is always to pay attention and to put one foot in front of the other.

We live in a "fix it" society, surrounded with countless ways of keeping ourselves so busy that we don't have time to sit still and experience what might be going on even just below the surface of our fast-paced thoughts and movement. The Ally's steady demeanor and confident voice are easily overshadowed by the chaos. Recently someone told me about being impatient with the microwave oven for taking a full three minutes to heat soup for lunch. Already the fact that the Internet gives us access to infinite information, products, and services is not enough; we must have faster access. It takes too long for that Web site to appear on my computer screen; I had better call the local cable company for service, so I can have rapid-fire access to the Internet twenty-four, seven.

I have no delusions about changing any of that. In fact, I accept that I am as caught up in life in the twenty-first century as anyone. I do like to remind myself that waiting for the microwave to heat my lunch or for the next Web site to appear is an opportunity for me to practice patience, but I am sure I will be signing up for faster access and buying computers with new, improved gizmos to make my relatively effortless life more effortless.

That same impatience, however, can create bigger problems in the arena of our personal exploration and growth. I have learned on numerous occasions (and I am certain I will learn this again) that my attempts to avoid dealing with any brand of emotional distress—be it fear, guilt, anger, sadness, or some combination of these—will only create more distress in my future. Emotions can only exist in the present. They cannot be left in the past, and they cannot exist in the future. Events and circumstances occur in the context of chronological time, but not emotions. Any emotional experience can only exist now. Either emotions are acknowledged and expressed or they remain with us into the next now.

Several years ago in a therapy group in which I was a client, I was talking about what I call the "principal's office syndrome," that feeling of dread that comes over me whenever I'm told that someone needs to "talk to me later." I have since discovered that many people share this experience, but on that day during group therapy my feeling was that I was very alone.

Jacquie, the group facilitator, asked me to describe the feeling of dread in more detail. "Where do you feel it in your body?" she asked.

"In the pit of my stomach," I said. "And in my throat. It's as if I'm going to either choke or throw up."

Jacquie stayed right with me. "Close your eyes and tell me where you see yourself. Try not to think about it. Just observe, and tell me what you discover." The exploration began.

With my eyes closed, continuing to feel what was becoming pain in my stomach and the increasing tightness in my throat, I was transported instantly back in time. "I am in the third grade. I remember my teacher that year because I had a crush on her: Mrs. Scuddy." I laughed. Scuddy did not seem like such an attractive name, I thought.

"Are you in Mrs. Scuddy's class right now, when you feel your stomach and your throat?" Jacquie asked.

I wasn't sure of the answer to her question. "It's like the answer is both—yes and no. That can't be . . . "

"Sure it can," Jacquie gently interrupted. "Just tell me where you are when you tune into the pit of your stomach and the choke in your throat."

Then I remembered what had happened. The morning bell had rung, and I was late for class. I started running up the stairs. The school principal, Mr. Simmons, called to me, "Young man!" I stopped dead in my tracks and turned around slowly. Mr. Simmons was a mean-looking man. That's how I remembered him that day in therapy, and that is how I remember him now as I write this.

Mr. Simmons called me to him. He was standing just outside the door to his office. As I walked toward him, he asked me if I remembered his recent announcement about not running in the halls. I, of course, admitted that I did remember. He pointed to a specific spot in the big hallway, just to the right of that door, and said, "You wait right here. I will be back in a few minutes." He was stern—no, he was mean and scary. I was eight years old, with terror in the pit of my stomach, and I felt as if I was going to throw up.

I remember Mr. Simmons walking away, down the hall and into another room. Then I was alone. Just me in that great big hallway, standing on the exact spot Mr. Simmons had assigned me. I stared at the doorway he had disappeared into. Then I turned my head and looked at the broad stairs, the steps that led to my third-grade class, and to Mrs. Scuddy. I have no idea how many times I looked back and forth between that doorway and those stairs or how long I remained there in that paralyzed state. I do know what I was thinking, though. I was measuring my chances of a getaway. If I could just get up those stairs and into my class, I felt sure I would be safe. There were so many classrooms and so many children in that building, after all. It would be virtually impossible for Mr. Simmons to find me.

I made my decision. I ran for it. I was already in trouble for running in the halls, but now I had to run as fast as I possibly could. I had to make it to the stairs, all the way up the stairs, and out of sight before Mr. Simmons reemerged from that doorway. I ran fast.

My classmates were still milling around, many out of their seats, when I got there, so it was not obvious I was arriving late. I quickly tried to blend in, also trying to conceal the fact that I was out of breath from my sprint up the stairs. I took my seat and pretended to review some spelling words that would be on a test later in the morning. (I was later amazed at how much vivid detail I recalled as I was describing these memories to Jacquie and the other group members.)

Just as I was beginning to feel relief, I looked up from my spelling words to see Mr. Simmons standing in the doorway. He was scanning the room, searching for me. I sunk low in my seat with my spelling list in front of my face in a futile attempt to avoid being caught. But of course he saw me. He crooked his finger toward himself, quietly reining me in. I cannot remember if Mrs. Scuddy was aware of this or not, but I do know that Mr. Simmons and I went back to his office alone, just the two of us.

"What happened in Mr. Simmons's office?" Jacquie asked.

"I sat there while he wrote my name in a little black notebook of his," I said. "He made it into such a big deal, definitely playing it over the top, enjoying his power over this little third grader." I could feel the anger begin to build as I described the scene to Jacquie.

I don't remember if he brought up the subject of paddling or I just thought on my own of the rumors I had heard about Mr. Simmons's "electric paddle," which of course did not exist. I do remember that once I was back in my classroom, I felt as though everyone was staring at me and think-ing bad things about me. I was certain that Mrs. Scuddy, my beautiful third-grade teacher, would be disappointed in me.

As I related this story to Jacquie and the group, the feel-ings in my gut and in my throat increased. Jacquie then helped me to create an imaginary scene in which I was able to travel back in time as an adult to protect my terrified third-grade self. Once I was able to feel the safety that the adult presence provided, the feelings in my gut and throat began to fly out of me. I screamed louder than I thought possible, and tears poured down my cheeks. I slammed my arms and fists into some big, safe pillows, as a combination of terror and rage continued to gush out. The group mem-bers gathered around close to support me. My third-grade self was no longer alone in that terrifying situation. Gradually the discomfort in the pit of my stomach dissolved and my throat became relaxed and open.

The emotions that were created when Mr. Simmons caught me running in the hall did not find expression at the time of the event. The event occurred in 1962, but as I iden-tified the source of my discomfort by telling the story in group therapy, the emotions did not exist in 1962. Those emotions were with me in that present moment. I felt that little eight-year-old boy's unexpressed terror in the present moment. This is the often painful work of *acceptance,* the third letter of our acronym map. When the blinders and the blindfolds are off, the emotions we discover must be felt if they are to be expressed. Once those stored emotions are expressed, however, they are gone.

Today, as I revisit the story of me and Mr. Simmons, I have no terror in my gut or tightness in my throat. I am drinking coffee and eating toast without the slightest inclination to throw up. I remember the emotions, but I do not continue to experience them. The memory of the terror and shame associated with this experience is a cognitive experience, in my mind rather than my gut.

I do still have feelings in the present moment associated with this story, however. They are feelings aroused not by Mr. Simmons or my desperate attempt to escape him, but feelings that accompany my thoughts on the subject. I feel compassion for myself at age eight, compassion for a little boy who felt so desperately alone. Depending on your personal history, you may or may not understand how such a seemingly trivial event would cause such distress, but that is beyond your or my control. The terror I have described is how I experienced that event in 1962. No amount of thinking could have ever changed that after the fact. But that is what we often fool ourselves into thinking: that we can reevaluate past events and, with benefit of new, improved thinking, we can change the emotions generated at that time of that event. We can't. We can influence how we will emotionally experience events in the future by changing how we think and how we interpret our world, but we can never change how we emotionally experienced something in the past. Once an emotion is created, it is with us and will remain with us, always in the present moment, until it is afforded opportunity for expression. We spend lots of time and energy trying to change the feelings that exist within us, but that is all wasted time and wasted energy. The work we are embarking on here will have nothing to do with changing the past, and it will have nothing to do with changing the emotions created in the past that we still carry with us. Our challenge is to find those unexpressed emotions—be they fear, shame, anger, or sadness—and offer them expression. Clear, honest, direct emotional expression is where healthy response begins.

One other present-tense emotion I associate with this childhood story, another feeling that, like the compassion, is not stuck within me, but created anew when I think about these events, is anger. It is probably better described as outrage. And it is a feeling that I do not want to run or hide from; it is what I consider the very appropriate feeling associated with thinking about adults in positions of authority, like Mr. Simmons, who (whether intentionally or out of ignorance) misuse that authority to frighten children. I will check later to see if Mr. Simmons is still alive. If he is, maybe I'll send him a complimentary copy of this book.

As cliché as it seems, most of the fears we will face in this process will have their roots in childhood experience. That doesn't mean that Mr. Simmons is the reason I have this feeling I call "the principal's office syndrome," although he certainly did inspire the syndrome's name. More likely, what this story points to are the fears and insecurities already existing in my eight-year-old consciousness. With benefit of lots of reflection, in and out of therapy, I can tell you that the deeper problem reflected in my "Mr. Simmons and me" story was that sense of aloneness I felt. As a child I learned to depend almost exclusively on "being good" for my sense of basic security and well-being. I did not know I could "get into trouble" and still be a good and acceptable person. I certainly did not know getting into trouble was normal for an eight-year-old. (Mr. Simmons, of course, did not seem to know—or care—that it is normal for an eight-year-old to run up stairs.)

Of course, exploring childhood stories is classic fodder for therapy, and like anything else it can be overdone. But the importance of discovering the unresolved feelings—even if not the events—from our past cannot be overemphasized. These are the sources for the ammunition the Bully uses to attack our self-esteem. These emotional experiences that we don't know what to do with are the places where we become stuck. This is where we need the third letter of our acronym map, *acceptance.*

When we become aware of these old, stored-up feelings, it is important to spend some time with them. Beware of tendencies to notice the feeling, quickly explain it to yourself, and then move on. I am not suggesting you become obsessive about your fears, just that you practice moving into that place of self-awareness without acting on the natural temptations to shut the feelings down, cover them up, minimize their importance, or explain them away. Some of the hardest work you will do will be sitting still with your fears, experiencing the anxiety or the terror sitting in the pit of your stomach or lodged in your throat. The effort to sit still and do nothing beyond being aware of a feeling state, even for just a few minutes, is real and difficult work. Please give yourself credit when you are able to do it, and try not to condemn yourself when you are not. I strongly urge you to make a decision right now to take plenty of self-compassion along on this journey.

In the short time I worked with Owen, he did some excellent work with unresolved feelings from childhood. Owen discovered he was essentially trapped between feelings of guilt and anger. He frequently used terms like "paralysis," "stuck," "nowhere to turn," "can't move," "no choice," and "immobilized."

He grew up witnessing his father control and mistreat his mother, his brothers, and himself. His father was constantly irritable, frequently explosive, and sometimes violent. The twist was that Owen's father blamed Owen for his dark moods and outbursts. There was no basis for the blame; Owen had simply been cast by his father as "the problem."

As we talked in therapy sessions about the impossible position he was put in as a child, Owen's emotional stuckness increased. The more specific he became about abusive scenes from childhood, the more outwardly calm he appeared. Of course, what appeared to be calmness was actually Owen's emotional paralysis.

The mistake I would have likely made earlier in my career would have been to prematurely explain everything I was seeing to Owen. It's not that explanation would not have been beneficial, but it would not have been the most helpful approach. The *E* in our acronym map does not stand for

Explanation and the *A* does not stand for Answers. The bigger challenge for Owen was to experience the emotions he originally could not have processed. He discovered that his anger and his guilt were locked in a sort of isometric tension, like pushing the palms of your hands together with all your strength. At an early age, he had begun condemning himself for being so powerless in the face of his family's problems, and as an adult he had continued to automatically cast himself in the role of "the problem."

Owen felt guilty because he was told everything was his fault and because he was helpless to change anything. He felt angry because that is a natural response to witnessing the abuse of innocent people and because his primary male role model—Dad—was always angry.

When he was invited (the child within given permission) to spend some time simply feeling all of the guilt and all of the anger, the isometric tension was released. Irony strikes again. By accepting each emotion, no matter how much has been stored up, competition between the emotions ("Am I angry or am I guilty?") ceased. Owen's frozen feelings thawed. He sobbed as the feelings of guilt poured through him, and the two of us stomped up and down together and screamed at the top of our lungs, expressing the old blocked anger. By asking nothing of himself other than to feel what he felt, Owen began to free himself from the guilt and anger that had held him for so long in that miserable, pseudocalm place.

Where's the fear in Owen's work? Everywhere. It is no stretch to figure out how frightened he must have been of his angry father, but the biggest fear we discussed was Owen's fear of his own blocked feelings. In one of our last sessions together, Owen said, "I didn't have the words to describe it before, but I have always been aware of the anger and the guilt piled up inside, and the thought of having to go anywhere near them scared me to death."

And on top of the fear, as so often is the case, was self-judgment. As I did Owen, I encourage you to suspend self-judgment as you read on. In our acronym map there is no *J* for judging. *Face* what you become aware of, whether it is in the form of a deeply ingrained fear or a seemingly innocuous complaint. *Explore* whatever you find, remaining willing to travel down the ladder to discover your deeper fears. And remember that *accepting* your discoveries and insights, contrary to popular belief, will not keep you stuck. Acceptance is the way through to the other side of your fears, where you will learn to *respond* from a position of power and strength.

Consider the emotions that may be stuck within you, the feelings still unexpressed. Be aware of the feelings. Resist the temptation to run, and resist the temptation to try changing whatever emotions you discover. Feel what is there to feel. Accept this as your experience, remembering that acceptance doesn't mean you like it; it only means you know that this is yours to experience.

Fully aware of these unexpressed feelings stuck somewhere inside you, try this strange little exercise: imagine that you, as an adult, can travel back in time, scoop up the child you once were, and walk right through the feelings. Repeat the motto to yourself: NO FEAR. Holding your child close to you, walk straight through the feelings, never changing one of them. Sadness, anger, hurt, shame, confusion—and all kinds of fear. Keep walking until you come all the way through.

The bad news—or what we think is bad news—is that we cannot change the feelings that are already inside us. The good news is that we don't have to change even one of them in order to heal. We simply have to become willing, with our eyes wide open, to walk straight through them.

CHAPTER FIVE

Why Me? Why Not Me?
The Question of Deserving

Hope and fear are traveling companions.

—T.R.

JUNE IS A THIRTY-SIX-YEAR-OLD successful corporate attorney with a long history of sexual abuse. Beginning at age four, she was sexually molested on a regular basis by several different adolescent boys and young men. This occurred in her own home, over a period of several years, and continued even after her mother became aware of what was happening. Consequently, June learned to abdicate her right to make her own decisions about sexual contact and continued to be involved in sexually abusive relationships as an adult.

June began therapy with me five years ago, several months after attending a local seminar I facilitated about overcoming depression. She had been in therapy a short time previously, but within three months of her initial visit, the psychologist she was seeing had begun making sexually inappropriate remarks, even suggesting that sexual contact between them would be beneficial to her therapy. Although she knew "something didn't feel right" about that situation, June did not discontinue therapy for several more months. She was successful in declining the psychologist's physical advances, although he continued to speak to her in sexually explicit terms, explaining that his approach was therapeutic. When she discontinued therapy with the psychologist, it was not because of his inappropriate behavior, but because she had begun a relationship with an extremely controlling man who insisted that he could not have a relationship with someone who was "mentally ill."

Over the course of the past five years, June has come to intellectually understand that the sexual contact she experienced as a child was inappropriate. Yet she continues to have difficulty referring to it as sexual abuse. "It just doesn't seem to be that big a deal," she says. This not an uncommon response, especially from survivors of such long-term sexual abuse. After all, sexual contact without her permission has always been the norm in June's life.

June has made significant progress in learning how to balance the professional and personal aspects of her life, and has begun recovery from an addiction to prescription medication. She has ended an abusive relationship and started a relationship with a man who loves and respects her. But the pain of betrayal by the people she loves the most—the betrayal of her parents who did not adequately protect her—still lies beneath the surface, out of June's sight most of the time. June continues to maintain that her history of sexual abuse does not seem to be "that big a deal."

When I first began to compare my own history with that of some of my clients, I had a problem. How could I justify being depressed to the point of suicidal thinking when I had first entered therapy, when so many people I treated had experienced so much worse? How could my story of getting in trouble for running in the school hallway compare to June's life of endless abuse? I had explored in-depth feelings about being disappointed and emotionally abandoned by my parents. I had talked about and analyzed my past, screamed at empty chairs, beat my fists and big foam bats on piles of floor pillows. Was I just that weak, that hypersensitive? If so, what right did I have to be there as June's therapist?

One of my clients had discovered the bodies of her parents following their murder/suicide; she was seven at the time. Another client lost her mother to cancer when she was four years old, and her mother was barely mentioned again as she grew up in a household with a stepmother who insisted on being called Mom. I have worked with clients who lost adolescent children to suicide. And I cannot count the number of clients who were physically and emotionally abused throughout childhood.

What I have learned is that this is not a simple matter of comparing what happened to me with what happened with June, or what happened with you. In fact, evaluating ourselves according to that kind of comparison is one extremely effective way of stopping forward progress dead in its tracks. I have heard this expressed in a very concise form: compare

and despair. Insisting on comparison as a way of either justi-
fying or denying our right to have pain is useless. We can
always find someone who has had it better than us and
someone who has had it worse. My childhood was better
than June's, but worse than someone else's. Even then, the
evaluation is subjective. I'm not sure June would agree that
my childhood was the better of the two.

You may have endured horrendous abuse in your life, or
you may be the product of the typical neurotic American
family. You are probably somewhere in between. It doesn't
matter. What matters is that we are all equally deserving of
whatever help we need in order to heal the wounds of our
past. And what matters is that we are all equally responsible
for tending to our own wounds.

What lies beneath the comparisons are the questions of
why me and not them or why them and not me. What lies
beneath those unanswerable questions are feelings of either
shame or anger. Maybe you feel shame because of your
abuse, or maybe you feel shame because someone else suffered abuse and you did not. You may be angry at your
abusers, or even angry at the fact that child abuse, in all of
its many forms and gradations, is a daily occurrence in our
world. But keep going. Climb down the ladder. Go beneath
the shame and the anger, and there it is again: fear.

We are afraid we might not deserve, might not be worthy
of the attention and the help we seek. We are afraid that if
we let ourselves acknowledge discomfort and pain, we will
succumb to our weakness. We are afraid—and taught to
believe—that any expression of dissatisfaction is only an

empty, impotent complaint. We are afraid of any number of things, including that if we look closely enough at our lives, we might discover our worst nightmare: meaninglessness.

Certainly I cannot offer you any guarantee that you will find meaning and purpose when you invest time and energy in examining your life. In fact, I tend to distrust those who tell me they know the specific purpose of their life—all tied up in a neat little package. I prefer the wisdom of Viktor Frankl, psychiatrist, author, and survivor of the Nazi death camps of World War II. Dr. Frankl tells us we should not ask, "What is the meaning of my life?" but instead realize that each of us is being asked, "What meaning will you make of your life?" It is an excellent question, possibly the only question we would ever need—a question I hope to never stop answering.

Put it to work and discover what a versatile tool it is. Ask the question about your life as a whole or apply the question to specific areas of your life. What meaning will I make of my life as a parent, spouse, friend, or worker? Or apply it to particular events or periods of time. What meaning will I make of my life in the wake of this disaster, or this loss, or this success? Probably the most powerful use of Frankl's excellent question is in daily practice. What meaning of my life will I make today? Use the question generously; it will certainly help you stay awake.

Listening to our dissatisfactions, discomforts, and pain will take us in positive directions too, as long as we know what to do with the information we gather. One of my favorite analogies is thinking of dissatisfaction as gasoline.

When we sit inhaling its fumes, nothing happens other than the destruction of brain cells, but when we put it to its proper use, it becomes powerful fuel that will take us where we want to go. We have been taught, instead, that dissatisfaction is the opposite of gratitude; that if we express dissatisfaction, we are being ungrateful. Consider how often the voice of dissatisfaction within you has been drowned out by the louder, shaming voice, accusing you of ingratitude. Consider how often other people have served as that louder voice, and how often you might have done the same for them.

All of this becomes a map of sorts, showing us the way toward the personal growth and enlightenment we seek. The map emerges when we learn to pay attention to everything: listen for the unanswerable questions ("Why me and not you, or you and not me?"), become aware of the anger or shame below the question, and the fear beneath the anger or shame. Fear's intent, though often misguided, is always protective. When you stand facing the fear, ask, "What are trying to protect me from? What is the danger you perceive?"

And when you ask a question of fear, become very still, sit quietly, and listen for the answer.

June sat in her usual seat. She leaned forward, her forearms resting on her knees, her hands clasped in front of her. The position—leaning forward—was my suggestion: a physical posture to help instill power and confidence. On this day she sat face to face with her fear. To the untrained eye, June sat facing an empty folding chair.

"Ask it what it is protecting you from," I prompted June, and she repeated the question to the empty chair.

June shifted into the folding chair, and answered in the character of her fear. "I am protecting you from yourself, the same as always." The voice is slightly different from June's usual voice, more monotone, flat, with a slight hint of impatience.

She moved back to "June's seat" to continue the dialogue. Long ago June had gotten over her self-consciousness about moving from chair to chair when having these conversations with herself. "I don't need you to protect me from myself. Maybe I did at one time. No, I'm sure I did before. But not now," June said.

"That's bullshit and you know it. I am here for your own good, and I'm not going to simply step aside because of your little therapy thing." (The inner voices we access in psychotherapy are frequently quite cynical and sarcastic about therapy, even when the client is enthusiastic about the process.)

Being more of a player-coach, I decided to join the conversation. Speaking directly to June's fear, I asked, "There is something here that you believe June cannot handle on her own, right?"

June was used to my participation in her inner dialogue. She responded in the character of fear. "You bet."

"What is it specifically that you believe she cannot handle?"

"The whole thing. She has never been any good at relationships. What makes her think she is anywhere close to being able to handle being married?"

"So you are going to sabotage the engagement, is that the plan?"

June's fear gives a slight shrug of the shoulders. "Yes, that would be the plan."

"Since you believe she will not be able to handle being married, you are going to do your best to end the relationship right now?"

"No, she doesn't have to end the relationship. I'm just here to keep her from making the mistake of getting engaged."

June suddenly moved to her usual seat; she had something to say to her fear. "This is my relationship. I will make the decisions about whether or not I get engaged. This is not up to you!"

I asked June, "You seem pissed off now. How does that feel?"

She paused, closed her eyes for a moment, then opened them. "At first I was going to say it felt bad, but that's not it really. Kind of good, or at least different. I don't know, it's weird."

June and I used the last few minutes of that session to accentuate her awareness of the anger that had spontaneously emerged in response to her overprotective fear. She had described the experience as "weird," a word I have come to recognize as indicative of progress in my clients. It felt weird because it was new. It was important for June to understand that "weird" in this case was good, not bad, as she had initially thought. Just when we begin to succeed in making the changes we seek, it is not unusual for another fear to emerge—the fear of the unknown, the fear of uncharted territory. For most of us, "familiar" is closely associated with feeling safe, even when what is familiar is an uncomfortable, isolating, or painful experience. When we are not vigilant about recognizing and maintaining our progress, and if we do not keep in mind that progress will initially feel "weird," we often fall back to familiar dysfunction as if doing so were dictated by the law of gravity.

When we feel afraid, we need reassurance. When we fear the unknown, two kinds of reassurance are available to us, and it is a good idea to have at least a little of each. The first kind of reassurance is the "I believe in you" kind. We feel this when someone we trust has confidence in us. It is not reasonable, or even desirable, to not need this kind of reassurance, but sometimes the cultural message that strength equals total self-reliance prevails, and we think it a sign of weakness to need reassurance at all. Strength is better defined as knowing when, how, and whom to ask for help, rather than the absence of needing help. Stubborn isolation, the refusal to allow anyone close to us in times of need, is not a show of strength. It takes far more strength—and courage—to reach out and let others in than it does to hide behind our walls of false bravado. Most of us need some "I believe in you" reassurance and an improved ability to let it in when it shows up.

To know that someone believes in you and believes in your ability to accomplish the task at hand is helpful, but it does not guarantee your success. This brings us to the second kind of reassurance needed as we prepare to face the unknown: the acceptance that there are no guarantees. This may seem misplaced or surprising when listed as a form of

reassurance, but we know it to be true. There are no guarantees. We hear it, and say it to the point it has become cliché.
Still we balk at the edge of new, unexplored territory, and
whether we admit it or not, there is at least a part of us waiting to be reassured with some guarantee of success.

After listening to the objections of June's fear of engagement and marriage, if I had told her that she didn't have
anything to worry about, that I was certain that she would
be able to "handle it," what effect would that have had? To
let her know that I do genuinely believe in her, and specifically in the progress she has made in therapy, will very likely
make a difference, but telling her I can predict the outcome
of her decision will only serve to reduce my credibility. I
would be claiming to be capable of doing something that we
both know I cannot. As her supporter, when my credibility is
lessened, even the power of my belief in her is diminished.

The most powerful stance any one of us can take when
we stand at the threshold of something new and previously
unexplored is best characterized as follows: gather the confidence you have in yourself, along with the confidence ("I
believe in you" reassurance) expressed by others, and plant
your feet firmly in the doorway of what is yet to come. Invite
your fear to speak. Do not hide from it; call it out. Look
directly at the fear, listen to what it is saying, what it is
threatening you with, and then take a deep breath and say,
"I'm willing to risk it."

"If you do this, you will be sorry," the Bully loves to say.

"I'm willing to risk it."

"You are sure to make a fool of yourself."

"Maybe. I'm willing to risk it."

"You can't do it. You have failed before, and you will certainly fail again."

"I have failed in the past and lived to tell the story. I am willing to risk it."

"This is it, your last chance. If you blow it this time, it's all over for you." The Bully is pulling out the big guns, the famous "last chance" threats.

And still you respond, "I doubt it, but even if that is so, I—am—willing—to—risk—it." See yourself speaking clearly and distinctly and, as you step across the threshold, push the fear aside with a powerful arm.

Watching this scene unfold never gets old, whether it is happening within a client's consciousness or we are literally acting it out in group therapy. "I am willing to risk it" is powerfully effective because it makes maximum use of the confidence we have in ourselves and that others have in us, plus it is a completely credible position. There are no guarantees, and we know it. Can I fail? Yes. Might I fail? Maybe. Will I hide or retreat? No. I am willing to risk it.

None of us is alone in this. Consider what we have in common. Regardless of our varied personal histories, we all experience dissatisfaction—small, medium, and large—and we all naturally react to that dissatisfaction. The important question is how we will react. One Nutshell on my wall speaks to this: "Don't waste your dissatisfaction; use it as fuel."

Fear is frequently the first to volunteer to lead such a reaction. Each of us can tell stories about inhaling dissatisfaction's fumes, times when we chose, consciously or not, to numb ourselves, distract ourselves, or fool ourselves into thinking that either nothing could be done or nothing needed to be done. These are our negative or evasive responses, led by fear. These are the times when we have hidden behind our perceived incompetence, rested too comfortably in our laziness, or taken refuge in our beliefs that we are not deserving of what we want in life. And in contrast we can all tell stories about dissatisfaction as fuel—the times in our lives when we responded proactively to the discomfort we felt and did not let fear stop us. These are times when we have moved toward the dissatisfaction rather than running or hiding from it. These are important times in our lives, frequently characterized by pain, but punctuated with positive change.

We all desire change, we all succeed in changing, and we are all self-contained with mechanisms that will sabotage that success. I told a client recently that for many years the unspoken motto of my life could have been, "It is not necessary for you to block my progress. Save your strength; I can do it myself."

Self-sabotage is simply a response to fear. Its intent, more often than not, is protective. June's fear told her to avoid moving closer in her relationship because she was not going to be able to "handle it."

Many of us respond to fear with avoidance. We take refuge in our potential. As long as there is something we are going to do (e.g., lose weight, stop drinking, write a book, change careers) in the future, we can safely perceive ourselves as potentially physically fit, sober, prolific, or successful in that new career. When we choose to take action toward a goal, the dream of our potential is in danger. By being proactive, taking the necessary risks, we have to face the comparison of our dreams to reality. We might fall short of our goals. We might fail. The prospect of such an outcome makes our potential seem like such a cozy place.

The perception of our potential is a very popular hideout. It is a place in our minds where procrastination reigns, where we keep ourselves sedated with pleasant images of all that we are bound to become and all that we will accomplish—later.

One of the distinct advantages of being an out-of-the-closet, recovering neurotic-depressive alcoholic psychotherapist is the ability to simply tell people how crazy I have been—and can be—as a way of offering them someplace to hang their own neurotic hats. We tend to think of ourselves as different from others, when in fact we are far more similar than dissimilar. Just as it was important for me to come to terms with my right to need help even though my personal history was not as severe as that of many of my clients', we all need to find that common meeting ground. It's called humility. One of the Nutshells defines it succinctly: "Humility is the awareness that I am neither better nor worse than anyone else."

We usually speak of humility in terms of not thinking too highly of ourselves. Nobody likes arrogance—except possibly the arrogant ones. And it is important to address tendencies toward an inflated ego, especially since arrogance is usually a cover for insecurity. Another of the Nutshells on my wall reads: "Arrogance can only exist where genuine self-love does not."

When it comes to accepting our similarities with others, another kind of ego problem often interferes. I call this problem "negative arrogance." This is the perception of ourselves as worse than others, less deserving, a self-imposed title of "Least Likely to Succeed." Negatively arrogant people have as unrealistic a view of themselves as the traditionally arrogant. Rather than thinking of themselves as better than others, the negatively arrogant underestimate their potential for positive growth and overestimate their destructive power. These are the people who will apologize incessantly, even when there is nothing to apologize for. And when you confront them with how irritating their constant apologizing is, they of course apologize.

The following is a creed for myself and my negatively arrogant brothers and sisters. If you identify, keep it handy to read now and then as a reminder of your "negative arrogance."

Admitting We're Wrong

We people of low self-esteem are so ready to be wrong. If something negative happens within a hundred-mile radius, we find a way to take the blame. "It must be me," we automatically assume.

If we are in conflict, and I am me and you are you, then I must be wrong . . . somehow.

But there is one subject about which we (people of low self-esteem) adamantly refuse to admit we are wrong. That subject is our own low self-worth. To this belief, that we are wrong, bad, and "less than," we hold so tightly that we couldn't possibly have space or energy for anything new—something new and radical, like feeling good about ourselves.

The truth is we are not bad or "less than." And we are wrong far less often than we have previously believed. But when it comes to this belief that we are worthless, we must . . . WE'RE WRONG! ADMIT IT!

Humility is the goal here, and it is not a minor goal. Humility is not just a pleasant character trait or a nice compliment. It is the necessary, realistic starting place for any of us who are serious about facing and conquering our fears. It is not reasonable to expect that we will stand up to our fears, resist the temptation of self-sabotage, set powerful sights on important goals, and accomplish those goals while holding on to an underlying belief that we are not as good or as deserving as others. To proceed in this way is as ridiculous as the alcoholic who tells me he wants to recover, but will not stop drinking, or the anorexic young woman who genuinely wants to feel better, as long as she doesn't have to gain any weight.

Humility is not humiliation. Humility is not shame. My father lived his entire life believing he was a failure. As a child, he was repeatedly told—in words and actions—that he was no good, that he always fell short of expectations, and that if something went wrong, it was certainly his fault.

My father was a kind man—to everyone but himself. Ironically, this is where he let me down. I grew up with a role model who was full of shame. He tried not to pass it on; to Dad's credit he was not shaming or critical as a parent. "Be happy," he would tell me. "Be proud of yourself." For this message I am grateful, but he left out an extremely important component of this lesson—he couldn't teach me how to be happy and proud of myself. Consequently, I became a man caught between knowledge and experience. I knew I was supposed to feel good about myself, and I was an expert at feeling ashamed of myself.

A few weeks before my father died, I had the chance to tell him that I had learned how to be proud of myself. "Not only that," I told him, "but I actually teach other people how to do it." I thanked him for what he had given me and told him I hoped he could feel some pride for the part he played in what I do for a living. I also wanted him to know that I was happy, that I had been able to dig myself out from under the shame that had haunted him for a lifetime and continued to cover him as he lay dying. In the bigger picture, my father has been my greatest teacher on the subject of self-compassion. As I listened to his words and watched him feel so undeserving of anything good in his life, I learned a valuable lesson. Dad told me what to do, and showed me specifically what would happen if I did not do it.

I recently talked about this aspect of my relationship with my father during a seminar on self-forgiveness. One of the participants questioned my use of the term "deserving."

"When you tell me I deserve good things," he said, "it

feels like you are letting me off the hook. It's as if you are saying I don't have to do anything to be deserving, as if the good things should just be handed to me on a silver platter."

"I see your point," I told the young man who had paid his money and wasn't about to let me off the hook. "A sense of deservingness without an accompanying sense of responsibility would be a problem. We've all known people with this problem. Some of us, of course, have been these people. They act as if they are entitled to things whether they work for them or not."

"Yes," another participant said, "and the person I think of who is like that has been in a lot of therapy. She seems to believe that if she sits around saying her affirmations, everything will just come to her."

"I know what you mean," I added. "I definitely went through a phase like that. Looking back, it is sort of like I was placing an order for health, wealth, and happiness as if it was pizza delivery: I'll have a positive, loving relationship—hold the mushrooms—and a couple hundred grand a year, with green peppers. How long will that take?

"I can even remember being really angry with a psychic I had consulted, because she had told me a lot of money was 'coming my way' and I had not seen any of that foretold prosperity. With hindsight, it is embarrassingly clear how I was side-stepping my own responsibilities, choosing instead to be upset with the psychic or angry with the universe for not providing as promised."

Believe it or not, I am always glad to have a couple of good skeptics in the group to challenge what I am teaching.

They generally bring out some very important points to help us keep our balance. Everything can be overdone, including self-help.

In response to the young man's challenge of my use of the term "deserving," there is a very important distinction to be made. And I find that distinction when I look back at Franklin Roosevelt's "four freedoms" speech. The freedoms President Roosevelt delineates—freedom of speech, freedom to worship, freedom from want, and freedom from fear—are not gifts to be delivered to each of us on silver platters or in pizza boxes. These freedoms are descriptive of our right to a fair and equal starting place, a universal "square one."

When I say we are all equally deserving, I do not mean we should reap the rewards for work we have not done. My intention is to confront those negative internal messages and beliefs about ourselves that tell us that we don't belong at "square one" with everyone else. I also want to be clear about my belief that without full acceptance of personal responsibility, deserving or not, we will not get to where we want to go.

Address these negative messages directly. Gather what you have learned so far and imagine yourself sitting face to face with the Bully. Speak the conversation out loud; give yourself permission to switch from one chair to the other to keep the personalities separate in your thinking. Or write a dialogue between yourself and the Bully.

And when you begin this direct dialogue—welcome to the final letter of our acronym map—you will now be in a solid position to choose your *responses* to fear.

CHAPTER SIX

Encore, Encore
Life's Recurring Themes

We fear something before we hate it; a child who fears noises becomes a man who hates noises.

—CYRIL CONNOLLY

"GOD FLUNKS NO ONE, but he sure does give lots of retests." So reads yet another Nutshell on my office wall. Haven't you noticed that certain themes have the nasty habit of popping up in our lives over and over again? Just when you think you have resolved the issue once and for all, there it is again, one of God's retests.

Sometimes the themes are specific fears that are repeatedly encountered, consistently there to stop us dead in our tracks. June's fear of involvement in a healthy relationship is a good example of a life theme that just won't go away. Kyle is a client whose recurring theme—a source of countless retests—is the challenge of overcoming mental and emotional paralysis when he is on the verge of success. Just as his hard work begins to show promise of paying off, the Bully steps in with a long list of reasons Kyle should reconsider his capacity to handle, and his deservingness of, the pending success.

Kyle describes it this way: "Just as I approach the door, put my hand on the doorknob, ready to finally step out into the success that at least part of me knows I deserve, the Bully clears his throat, and says, 'Do you really think this is such a good idea, Kyle?'"

The Bully's outwardly simple question is full of booby traps. Kyle, suddenly consumed with fear in the form of self-doubt, turns back around and sits down to listen to the Bully's list of things to fear.

Discovering our greatest fears is not the goal of personal growth, or at least it is not the ultimate goal. As crazy as it sounds, however, searching for those fears is an important part of the process. Recurring fears are clues. When we encounter fear, our reflex tendency is naturally to run the other way. That is what fear tells us to do, after all. But a commitment to personal growth calls for a different choice, a choice to actually search for and examine our fears, especially recurring fears. They are important clues in our intrapersonal investigation.

President Roosevelt told us that the only thing we have to fear is fear itself. The NO FEAR motto reminds us that we must face our fears. Our acronym map tells us that we don't get rid of recurring fears; we move toward them, experience them, and move past them. The strange but good news is that the fears themselves don't have to change at all. Fear is not the problem. It is our relationship to the fear that determines the choices we make. By changing our relationship to fear, we reduce its credibility, robbing it of its power to stop us. It's sort of like demoting your fear, busting it down to a lower rank. Maybe the only thing we have to fear is the fear of fear; maybe that's what FDR meant.

In the spirit of organization, consider three categories of recurring life themes: *fear themes, obstacle themes,* and *themes of personal desire. Fear themes* are straightforward; the Bully tells us exactly what to be afraid of. No tricks, just good old-fashioned bullying. "You never were any good at speaking in front of a crowd," the Bully might say. "You are probably going to make a fool of yourself tonight." Or the Bully might say, "Relationships are for other people, people who can handle them, not for you." Or "It doesn't even make sense for you to put in for that promotion. You won't stand a chance, and on the off chance you did get the position, you wouldn't know what to do with it."

Obstacle themes are patterns of thinking, mechanisms of our own construction, that we get caught up in and can't get beyond, keeping us blocked from forward progress. Themes of personal desire are those things that are most important to us relative to who we are; what holds meaning for our lives: our dream, our passion, our calling. At first glance, these two other categories of recurring life themes appear to be Bully-free. But they boil down to the same substance: fear. So learning to recognize obstacle and personal desire themes in our lives is an important way to become aware of the work we have to do to overcome fear's control. Our acronym map and the climbing-down-the-ladder technique work effectively with all three theme categories.

Steven needed people to "understand" him. We all want to be understood, but Steven's perceived need for understanding was so extreme that it became an obstacle to his forward progress. To compound the problem, Steven seemed to especially need understanding from people when they were upset with him. It is amazing how clever we can be when it comes to setting ourselves up for disappointment.

I asked Steven what he thought was so important about being understood.

"I don't know. It just feels bad when I'm not."

I guided Steven down the ladder to find something more helpful.

"If someone doesn't understand me, then . . ." I began.

"Then they think I'm wrong," he responded immediately.

"If someone thinks I'm wrong . . ." I continued.

"If I'm wrong . . ." Steven paused for a moment, and I interrupted.

"No, I didn't say 'If you are wrong.' I said, "If *someone thinks* you are wrong."

He looked confused, as if to say, "What's the difference?"

Sometimes we will discover something very significant just one or two rungs down the ladder. That was the case with Steven. Or maybe the more accurate application of the metaphor is that Steven skipped several rungs and went directly to "being wrong." When someone was upset with him, which we later discovered meant that they had an opinion that differed from Steven's, without giving it any thought Steven discounted his own perspective. Steven would continue to fight for understanding, trying to gain the other person's understanding (i.e., validation via agreement), but not because he thought he was right. Steven had been told he was wrong so consistently as a child that he unconsciously believed that he could be "right" only with the specific validation of others. As long as anyone did not understand him—again, this turned out to be more about validation and agreement than traditional understanding—Steven was wrong.

His obstacle theme was about "being wrong" and turned out to consist of a series of blocks in the form of erroneous judgments of himself. Beneath the judgments Steven and I discovered, as is often the case, a deep fear of being rejected and left alone.

Helping Steven to realize how he was giving others so much authority over his self-image would certainly have been helpful to him in and of itself, but he was able to experience a deeper healing by tracking down the fears beneath his obstacles.

An obstacle that has circled back on my wife, Dede, through the years is that of having difficulty identifying her own emotional needs in times of increased stress. Many of us have obstacle themes associated with self-neglect and self-sabotage, but beneath them all are our fears. The closer we come to identifying our deepest fears, the more powerfully we are able to break through our obstacles, and put an end to—or at least reduce the frequency of—the retests.

Walter was fifty-two when we met. He was participating in a dream-interpretation seminar I cofacilitated with my friend and colleague Hillary Ellers. Walter was articulate, insightful, and funny. He seemed to enjoy and benefit from the exercises and the discussion over the course of the day-long event, and his responses to other participants demonstrated keen perception and genuine empathy. Shortly after the dream seminar, Walter called my office and made an appointment.

What quickly became apparent was that Walter was an absolute veteran of psychotherapy and a multitude of personal-growth philosophies, programs, products, and services. He spoke of transactional analysis, gestalt, codependency, bioenergetics, rebirthing, past lives, primal scream, and holotropic breathing. The man was extremely knowledgeable, to the point that I felt intimidated at times.

As a result, our first half dozen sessions or so were stimulating, intellectual conversations. I made some decent attempts to pinpoint some specific reasons why he had showns up for therapy at this time in his life, but my attempts rolled off Walter like the proverbial water from a duck's back. Walter sort of rambled aimlessly, in no particular direction, with no identifiable themes.

I decided that if I was going to earn my pay in Walter's case, I needed to push a little harder to find out what he wanted from therapy. Early in one session I got that particular ball rolling.

"Walter, we have been meeting on a weekly basis for a

couple of months now, and I've got to tell you, although I have thoroughly enjoyed our time together, I still haven't got a clue what you want from me."

He seemed taken off guard, momentarily confused. And I'm pretty sure I saw at least a slight flash of anger in his eyes. But within five seconds, Walter had shifted in his chair, uncrossed and crossed his legs, and he was back in the saddle again. He responded with a joke. "I want to be healed— healed from head to toe. I thought you knew that."

"Of course, item number 248 on the therapy menu: complete healing. But specifically what would that mean for you—to be healed?"

That was my move to go beneath his joke, to see if I could get us onto a more productive track.

The silence that followed my question to Walter was brief, but it was enough to tell me we had successfully made a transition. He was giving my question some thought.

"I don't know," Walter said, his voice a little softer than usual. "What do you think it means?"

"It's a very subjective question," I told him. "I'm interested in what you think right now."

"Spoken like a true therapist." Walter smiled. "I'm going to have to give it some thought."

"Definitely, give it some thought. This is the kind of question to which there are many answers. I call them 'magnet questions,' important questions that you can carry around with you, allowing them to attract various responses over a period of time. But for starters, right now, right here,

what comes to mind when you consider the question? Close
your eyes, repeat the question to yourself: 'What would it
mean for me to be healed?'"

Walter closed his eyes and sat more quietly than I had
ever seen him. With his eyes still closed, he said, "It would
mean that I know who I am, and that I would know what I
am here for."

"So, who are you? What are you here for?"

"Now I'm the one who hasn't got a clue," Walter said.

On a bookshelf in my cluttered therapy room is a small
clay jar with a label that reads "Tough Questions." That jar
sits next to the one that reads "Ashes of Problem Clients,"
both gifts from a client I worked with many years ago. I am
glad to report that the "Ashes" jar is empty. Inside the
"Tough Questions" jar, however, is a small slip of paper with
a single question written on it: "What the f—k is going on
here?" I have no idea who put the question in the jar, but it
is a good one. Corny, cliché, or trite as it may sound, good
psychotherapy often does come down to asking those exis-
tential questions. "Who am I?" "What is my purpose?"
"What the f—k is going on here?"

For Walter, this level of introspective questioning began
after many years of various therapies, hundreds of self-help
books, and dozens of seminars and intensive workshops, when
the two of us found our way past both of our senses of humor,
and specifically past one particular sentence that we at first
assumed was only a joke. "I want to be healed," Walter said.

Frequently the turning points in our lives are those times
when someone or some circumstance or occurrence inter-

rupts our "business-as-usual" daily grind to pose a simple question or two. "What is going on here?" "Who am I?" "Is there a purpose to all this?" "And if so, what could it be?" If we stop at the level of intellectual discussion, and certainly if we just laugh it off, we might remain safe, protected for the time being from these deceptively simple, yet disturbing questions. One of the many things I love about what I do for a living is the opportunity I have to point to those questions as I work side by side with people, sorting through their psyches as if we are cleaning out the garage after many years of expert procrastination.

Remember, my theory is that God made me a therapist so I would be in lots of therapy. There is no way I can effectively guide others to identify and face these questions in their lives without consistently revisiting them in mine. I don't pretend to have the answers to the questions, although there have been times when I thought I caught a glimpse—from the corner of my eye, just a quick movement of an elusive answer as it ducked around the corner before I could turn to look. At this point in my life, I have come to believe that from the human perspective—a severely limited view of universal existence—finding the answers is not nearly as important as discovering the questions, that holding them up to the light will serve to keep us awake, alert, and at least in search of a purposeful path.

Walter and I discovered that one big obstacle theme for him was ironically his nonstop pursuit of personal growth. When I was thinking that Walter was rambling aimlessly, I was not seeing the forest for the trees. The theme I was missing was Walter's pursuit of personal growth without any identifiable goals. Like recurring fear themes, obstacle themes in our lives are clues, put there to get our attention, intrigue us, and ultimately to guide us toward the Bully. As long as Walter remained occupied with all the various brands of therapy, self-help, and personal-improvement techniques, there would be no space in his consciousness for him to have to experience what he and I discovered was his greatest fear: that he might be a man without a purpose.

Discovering and standing up to Walter's biggest fear naturally led his work in therapy to focus on themes of personal desire, the third category of recurring life themes. This is often the case: when we seek out our fears and listen to what they have to say, we can clearly identify themes of personal desire obviously imbedded in the expression of the fear. My wife's fear that we would not be able to remain on our farm expresses the importance of her connection to the animals she loves so dearly. And for Walter, his fear of being useless became the catalyst for his search for personal meaning.

Themes of personal desire are not so much recurring as they are constant. These themes are continuous; we just lose touch with them at different times throughout our lives. Sometimes themes of personal desire are long-forgotten dreams, and the task is to reconnect and find permission (from within) to explore the possibilities of helping the dreams come true. My father shared with me that he wanted to be a forest ranger, but did not pursue that path because his father insisted that he go into the family business. Even though my father never allowed himself to follow his dream, his desire to be a forest ranger remained constant throughout his life. He told me a few weeks before he died that his fear of failure had kept him from taking the risk. Ironically, and very sadly, my father died believing he was a failure anyway.

We are all influenced by themes of personal desire, but not everyone identifies them. Unfortunately, we often don't find our way beyond the perpetual recurrence of obstacles and fears. Too often we live our lives by default rather than decision. We accept beliefs and value systems that are handed to us, allowing life's circumstances to determine the directions we will take without realizing that what we do with our lives is up to us. The idea that personal desires are not only important but central to living fully and responsibly often seems ridiculous, idealistic, naive, or selfish. My father lived like this—a good man who never believed he could be in charge of his own life. I believe he was happy to learn that I had escaped the prison mentality that had shaped his self-image, but I am sure he never saw the same opportunity for himself.

Walter encountered one particular obstacle in his pursuit of purpose that is important to mention because it represents a common misconception that frequently slows progress. That obstacle is the assumption that our purposes in life are assigned to us, rather than chosen by us. I cringe a little each time I hear someone say, "I want to know what my purpose is," or in response to a specific situation, "I wonder what I am supposed to learn from this." These statements limit us severely by implying that there is some kind of "answer in the back of the book," the one correct answer to the question. The more productive questions to ask are, "What do I want my purpose to be?" and "What are some things I can learn from this situation?"

Sometimes connecting with themes of personal desire becomes the catalyst for grieving. Bailey is a fifty-three-year-old woman who has never married and had children. She began therapy two years ago for severe depression. Bailey has overcome her depression and has just recently "remembered" how important her dream to have children had been to her as a young adult. The opportunity for the dream as she dreamed it has passed, and for that she is grieving. I expect that as Bailey emerges from her grief, we will be talking about creating an alternative to her original dream—adoption, foster parenting, working with children as a teacher or mentor, and so on.

This is often the case when someone successfully resolves the initial crisis that brought them to therapy. If the person remains in therapy after the smoke clears—personal desire themes are likely to surface. A very important question appears: "What had I intended for my life?"

Ask yourself this question: "What had you intended for your life?"

When we fail to ask ourselves this question, we may simply live our lives out by default, nudged this way and that by life's circumstances, forgetting that we ever had a plan for our lives at all. Or we may devote our lives to what I have come to think of as mistaken personal desire. Jenni is a good example of someone who almost devoted her life to a mistaken personal desire.

Jenni dreamed of being a doctor—or so she thought. In college, she spent every moment either studying, volunteering in hospitals, or leading extracurricular organizations—shaping herself into the perfect medical-school applicant. The perpetual fear of failure controlled her and would never leave enough energy or time to ask, "Is this really what I want to do with my life?" Only after she was accepted into medical school did she stop and consider what she truly desired. Because she no longer had to prove herself to the medical-school acceptance committees, she didn't have to study quite as hard, volunteer quite so many hours, or lead quite so many campus meetings. In short, the Bully lost his tight grip. Jenni finally took the time to pay attention and listen to the voice of healthy fear.

The Ally came to the rescue. Jenni described it to me in one session.

"It was like a strong, loving voice from deep within me, saying, 'Jenni, I am afraid you are going to let your dream go. The real dream. Your dream.'"

Jenni's "real dream" is to pursue a career as a songwriter and recording artist. She is as talented musically as she is intelligent academically, but somewhere along the line her dream had taken a backseat to the dream she believed her parents had for her and the dream that one particular pre-med professor had for her. She became convinced that a career in medicine was the only way she could be of service to others and that her desire for a career in music was selfish and unrealistic.

Today Jenni is pursuing her music career in Nashville, Tennessee.

It is only natural to our human condition that we will revisit themes from all categories, most likely for the duration of our lives. The lesson here is to let go of any unrealistic ideas about getting rid of these recurring themes. Perfectionistic thinking like this will only turn out to be one more obstacle standing between us and the people we want to be.

Perfectionism is a serious and pervasive problem leading us in the opposite direction from where we need to go. It is perfectionistic thinking that misleads us into thinking we are supposed to completely destroy all obstacles in our paths and never lose site of our personal desires; and it tells us the even bigger lie: we are supposed to banish all fear.

When the themes recur, it may mean we have not been making progress and are in need of retesting. The problems related to my drinking were bound to recur as long as I failed to acknowledge my alcoholism. If you have a history of being in one abusive relationship after another, it certainly may mean you are hiding your head in the sand when it comes to accepting responsibility for yourself.

But sometimes the recurrence of our themes is not a retest. We may be revisiting our themes because it is time to learn the next lesson. After all, the engineer doesn't express surprise that each successive year of education continues to involve mathematics. The law student expects to study law. The carpenter's apprentice has made a choice to learn carpentry.

I think we are like the engineer, the law student, or the

carpenter's apprentice. Maybe the themes we identify as recurring in spite of our previous efforts and progress are simply indicative of the course of education we have chosen for our lives. Maybe not. But regardless of how or why the themes came to be, to proceed as if they are our chosen lessons is an effective approach to life.

Our particular recurring themes are apparently beyond our choosing. What we do choose, however, is whether or not we will become aware of the themes, and whether or not we will accept responsibility to learn their lessons. Just being enrolled in school or even just showing up for class does not ensure a passing grade.

When we encounter our life themes, we must remember what we have learned. If faced with a recurring fear, we can immediately put our acronym map to work. When considering obstacle themes or themes of personal desire, we must first find out where the Bully is hiding. We do this by asking questions. We might try climbing down the ladder. After we find the fear, we must see it for what is, walk toward it, and then past it. We change our relationship with the fear and take charge of our lives.

Make a list of a few recurring themes in your life. See if you can think of an example from each category. Maybe there is one life theme you have significantly resolved, such as a dysfunctional relationship pattern or, like Jenni, a career direction. Maybe there is a life theme you have just recognized as you read this chapter. Or maybe one particular life theme has been haunting you for as long as you can remember.

Keep in mind that we are all works in progress. Accept the fact that we are imperfect human beings who will be experiencing these themes for the duration of our lifetimes. This is an effective way of pacing ourselves so that we don't become exhausted, approaching personal growth as if it is a race to the finish line or some kind of finite project to be completed so we will have some time to spare.

Walter was in my office not long ago for what he called a "check-up" session. He discontinued our regular meetings a little more than two years ago. Since then I had heard from him three or four times via e-mail, and I knew he started a new company with the mission of helping people with career dissatisfaction explore creative options for rediscovering a sense of purpose in their lives. No accident there. Before leaving therapy, Walter told me he wanted to share what he had been discovering with other people, specifically with the people he called the "aimless ones."

"Going without therapy for the last couple of years has been very therapeutic," Walter said.

"What have you been doing with all that time, energy, and money you were spending on your perpetual psychological makeover?" I asked.

"The biggest challenge has been remembering that I don't always have to be doing something. But I have to admit, the new business is keeping me pretty busy."

"Busy? How busy?" Walter and I had spent considerable time working on his compulsive need to constantly be doing something. Even after he had let go of the myriad of personal-growth pursuits, new activities and projects seemed to spring up from every corner of Walter's life.

"Probably past the point of being healthy some of the time. A lot of the time. Most of the time. That's the not so good news. But the great news is that I absolutely love what I am doing. I am really on the right track. Who would have guessed that I would find purpose in helping others find purpose?"

"You're right, that is excellent news," I said. "Do you want to talk about the possibility that, in spite of your maintaining that important sense of purpose, you are repeating an old pattern here?"

"What old pattern?" Walter asked.

"Staying so busy you don't have time or space to know what is really going on with yourself. That old pattern."

Walter paused, considered my suggestion, then nodded his head slightly. "Oh, that old pattern."

I haven't seen Walter since that session. If we want to be judgmental, we could make the argument that Walter is avoiding work on his compulsive busy-ness, that this particular obstacle theme has come to call and Walter is refusing to answer the door. If we want to be generous, we could make the argument that by not "working on" his compulsive activity, he is demonstrating growth beyond his previous hypertherapeutic behavior. If we want to be accurate, we could take the middle ground position that there is probably some truth in each of these assessments. If we want to be fair, we could realize that this is really none of our business.

It's one thing to tell the story of Walter, or of June, or of you or me for the purpose of learning a little something about ourselves; but we must be careful not lose sight of the subjective nature of these stories. What we decide to be aware of, attend to, and work on are personal choices, choices that are a significant part of who we are as individuals. How I approach a situation in my life may or may not be similar to your approach. How I approach a situation today is likely to be very different from how I would have approached a similar situation ten years ago. It's only reasonable to assume that my approach in five years will be different as well. Healthy personalities are fluid, not stagnant, and when we respect that—in ourselves and in each other—we realize that psychotherapy and self-help material will benefit us most when it is tailored to fit our individual personalities and needs. Carl Jung said that he developed a new therapy for each of his patients. My client Jenni said that she thought of therapy as collaborating with me to write her own personalized self-help book.

Remember that no matter how much we may have in common, we are individuals, with the right and responsibility to decide for ourselves how and when to address these continuing life themes. This is essential in developing genuine respect for ourselves and for each other.

Respect. Isn't that what it is all about? What greater compliment can be paid than "He respects, and is respected by others"? Earning our own respect is often the greater challenge, though. And since respect for others begins with self-respect, isn't that one life theme we all have in common?

CHAPTER SEVEN

Unique Just Like Everyone Else

What We Have in Common

You gain strength, courage and confidence by every experience in which you really stop to look fear in the face. . . . You must do the thing you think you cannot do.

—ELEANOR ROOSEVELT

FEAR TAKES MANY FORMS: dread, worry, panic, anxiety, self-consciousness, superstition, negativity. And it shows itself in many ways: avoidance, procrastination, judgment, control, agitation, perfectionism. These are just some of the guises of fear.

If negativity were an Olympic event, I would be from a family of gold medalists. I grew up with an ever present sense that no matter how successful I might be now, the next step was bound to be my doom. In elementary school, I was a straight-A student, but I would stay awake nights before a big test, literally becoming physically ill, because I was certain I was going to fail. My fear was not that I would make a B or even a C. And I didn't think of it as a fear. I experienced it as a certainty: tomorrow the bottom would finally drop out, and I would fail.

In preparation for writing this book, I flipped through some of my old journals written over the past many years. Not surprisingly, it was not difficult to find a few entries about fear:

It seems that fear and hope are traveling companions. For me anyway, hope seldom travels alone.

Fear must not sleep much. Lately it is talking to me when I fall asleep, and still talking when I wake up in the morning.

We all want a life like aluminum siding—with a guarantee.

A rhyming Nutshell: "Hear with your ears, rather than your fears."

How much more relaxed would I be, how much more my true self, how much more productive and efficient and effective, how much more loving and generous and focused would I be ... if this fear didn't live in my chest?

No matter what our personal recurring life themes may be, when you put them in the kettle on the stove, they will all boil down to fear. It's what we all have in common. We will experience fear in different ways, depending on more variables than we could possibly count, and we will respond to fear in our own ways. There is no escaping the fact that fear is a universal experience that we share not just with other human beings, but with all creatures. Sometimes I think the primary difference between how my dog and I experience fear is that he tends to be afraid when there is legitimate danger, while I have the capacity—and the inclination—to scare myself with my highly evolved mind in the absence of any real threat.

One of my journal entries asks the question, "How might I be different if this fear did not live in my chest?" It's a good question. We need to ask such questions in order to challenge ourselves to keep moving—specifically to keep moving in a direction of our own choosing. My friend Jana Stanfield, an inspirational speaker, songwriter, and performer, asks a similar question in her song "If I Were Brave":

If I refuse to listen to the voice of fear,
would the voice of courage whisper in my ear?

And the chorus of Jana's wonderful song poses a question we can all use:

If I were brave I'd walk the razor's edge,
where fools and dreamers dare to tread,

and never lose faith, even when losing my way.
What step would I take today if I were brave?
What would I do today if I were brave?

Brave Faith (1999)

And that is the best way I know to proceed. Since we are not going to outrun fear, or outsmart it, or successfully hide from it, we wake up each morning and ask ourselves Jana's question: "What would I do today if I were brave?" And then, to the very best of our ability, we go do just that. Remember our motto: NO FEAR. I honestly believe that when we can refuse to abide by the voice of fear, the voice of courage will whisper into our ear.

Easier said than done, you say? And I answer yes, much easier said than done. At that moment in time when we decide to stop running, stop hiding, and stop trying to outwit our fears, we are only at the very beginning, the starting line. Most of us travel quite a distance just to get there.

A decision is a beginning, and it is a choice of direction. Deciding to face our lives with courage and integrity is analogous to saying I plan to stop drinking, I plan to exercise regularly, or I am going to travel from California to North Carolina. The decision will not get us sober, a health club membership will not get us in shape, a chosen direction will not make the trip for us.

The best definition for wisdom is the increasing awareness of all that we do not know and all that we do not control. As these two lists continue to grow, I have become more comfortable not knowing and not controlling. At one point in my life, any comfort at all with this awareness would have been impossible. It would have been too threatening to my ego to acknowledge my lack of control of the world around me or to admit all that I do not know. Regarding this matter as of today—right here, right now—I am, of course, a work in progress. In the midst of my ever increasing awareness of what I do not know, however, I have come to accumulate a small list of what I consider "knowns" when it comes to myself and others involved with personal-growth work.

These "knowns" are points of information that can make a tremendous difference when it comes to facing and conquering our fears. They are simple truths about ourselves that, once acknowledged, offer us a way of creating a plan, keeping us unstuck, on track, and moving in our chosen directions. These simple truths help us to see the Bully as separate from ourselves and tell us that it is our decision to face him. They tell us to expect resistance and then encourage us to do whatever it takes to overcome our fears. These simple truths are what I have come to think of as "offensively simple," ideas we tend not to question much, ones we are likely to pass over as "obvious." All too often we fail to give them the attention they deserve. It seems inherent in our human condition that we overlook the simple in the search for something more complex. I think that this is a version of the "medicine has to taste bad to be good" mentality. It is the Serenity Prayer applied backward again: our efforts going to things we can't change, ignoring the simple things we can. Well, medicine does not have to taste bad, and most of the time simple is more powerful than complex.

Let's look at the myth of singularity a little more closely. Consider the times in your life when you have faced big decisions—decisions about relationships, jobs, or family. Have your decisions always been easy? Have you always known just the right thing to do? In times of decision, do you tend to be single-minded, or are you aware of "the inner committee" voicing at least a contradictory point of view, if not several different perspectives? And have you ever felt "crazy," "stupid," or some other negative characterization because you were experiencing your multiple nature?

A friend of mine teaches a communication course at a local college. He begins each semester by asking his class, "How many of you talk to yourselves?" My friend tells me that anywhere from 75 to 90 percent of the class will raise their hands. Then he says, "Of those of you who did not raise your hands, how many thought to yourself, 'Do I talk to myself? I don't think I talk to myself . . . '" The point is obviously that we all talk to ourselves.

Once the idea of relationship within a single mind is accepted, we become aware that there is more than just a single-parent family (adult and inner child) living inside. For years I have been talking with my clients and speaking to audiences about the Ally, the Bully, and the rest "the committee within." I never have to spend more than a minute or two explaining what I mean. We all have these inner committees. The challenge is to stop pretending that we don't, and to stop believing we are crazy simply because we carry on conversations with ourselves. It is time to step into the conference room where the committee works and take charge.

When you take your place at the head of the conference-
room table, ready to address your committee, ready to claim
your rightful authority over this domain, you will probably
feel anything but powerful and anything but prepared. At
that precise point, when you feel the power draining away
and self-doubt surrounds you, give yourself credit for showing up at all. And try your best to hang on to this little reassurance: you do have what it takes, and you will take
charge—of your committee, and of your life.

Therapeutic work that has been done with the concept of
discovering the wounded child within us is an excellent way
to think "multiple." The metaphor of the inner child has
been so widely used that it has become cliché, as evidenced
by the popularity of comedian Al Franken's parody character
Stuart Smalley. When a concept becomes cliché, it
inevitably loses some of its usefulness, but it is important in
this case that we not throw the inner child out with the
bathwater. The essential value of this metaphor is that it
offers a context in which we can tangibly perceive our individual selves in terms of relationship. Within that relationship context, we can better understand our multiple nature,
and we are in a better position to accept full responsibility
for ourselves.

I am usually the first one to laugh at psychobabble, or
something that seems too contrived, in a therapeutic setting.
In fact, I recently angered a client when I mentioned that I
thought a therapy assignment I was giving to her and her
husband was corny. I explained to her that corny does not
mean ineffective. Sometimes in personal-growth work we

have to put up with the corny and contrived, a little like tolerating side effects of a medication that is effective. Similarly, if the side effects prove worse than the benefit of the medication (or technique), then it is time to move on to the next option.

A simple example of the power of the inner-child metaphor can be seen in my work with Sam, a forty-five-year-old man who came to therapy because of a long history of depression in conjunction with compulsive overeating. I asked Sam to bring a photograph of himself as a child to his next therapy session. The next session, he brought a black-and-white photograph of himself at age three or four, in a beautiful antique picture frame. The photograph and frame had belonged to his father, who had died several years earlier.

"In spite of the fact that I tend to completely avoid thinking of my childhood, this picture and frame are special to me because they belonged to my father," Sam told me.

I placed the photograph on a table next to me, facing Sam, as we continued our conversation. Later in the session, when we were identifying a number of Sam's strongly self-critical thoughts, I asked for a clarification. "So you tell yourself repeatedly that you are fat, worthless, and lazy, is that right?"

"Among other things," Sam said.

"So you could say to yourself right now, 'Sam, you are fat, worthless, and lazy'? Is that right?"

Sam looked at me as though I might be having trouble hearing, but responded again, "Yes, that would be no problem."

I suggested the simplest of therapeutic exercises: "I want you to look directly at the photograph of yourself at four years old and imagine that the little boy in the picture is sitting in this room with us now. Okay?"

"Okay."

I continued. "Now I want you to look directly at the little boy—little Sam—and say to him, 'Sam, you are fat, worthless, and lazy.' Okay?"

He looked at the photograph as I had instructed, but he said nothing. In fact, he didn't move at all. He didn't seem to be breathing. The instruction had paralyzed him.

I nudged Sam some more. "Go on, say the critical statement to the little boy."

More stillness and silence. Then Sam said, "I don't think I can."

"What do you mean you don't think you can? You just told me that you would have no problem telling yourself here and now that you are fat, worthless, and lazy. I am just asking you to say that sentence in the direction of the little boy."

"I don't think I can say it to him."

"Okay," I said, changing the exercise slightly, "then forget about imagining little Sam in the room with us. Just say it to the photograph. Just say, 'Sam, you are fat, worthless, and lazy.'"

Sam's eyes had been fixed on the photograph, but now he looked up at me. Corny, contrived, or not, he had tears in his eyes when he said, "Thom, I can't do it. That kid doesn't need one more person putting him down, telling him that crap."

Sam and I had worked together long enough for him to know that I was playing devil's advocate now, so I continued. "Crap? What do you mean, crap? You told me that you believe that so-called crap."

"I do believe it. I am fat, worthless, and lazy. There, I said it," Sam said with authority in his voice. He seemed almost proud to have proven his point. But, of course, he had not proven any point.

"Okay, so you believe it. It is the truth. Say it to the little boy."

"No. I can't say it to him." Sam's voice was softer again.

"Is it true about him?" I asked. "Is little Sam fat, worthless, and lazy?"

"I don't know. That's what I always thought."

"Are you saying that was what little Sam always thought? Did little Sam grow up believing that he was fat, worthless, and lazy?" I asked.

"Yes, definitely," Sam replied, looking back again at the photograph.

"Well, what do you think? Not about you, but about him. What do you think about that little boy? Is he fat, worthless, and lazy?" I was pushing a little because we were definitely getting somewhere.

"No, he's just a kid. He's just four years old," Sam said, shaking his head slightly, sounding partially confused, but mostly sad.

Sam left that session with something very tangible that he had not previously had: a way to experience genuine self-compassion. This came about, as it has for many of us, when he could see himself in the context of relationship. When Sam could see himself as the adult in a relationship with his inner child and see that his negative self-talk was actually directed at that child, he felt something he had not felt before. He felt love and compassion for a part of himself.

The metaphor of an inner child in Sam's case, and with any number of the rest of us, makes it possible to begin practicing self-compassion. We can do it without having to wait for the unanimous committee vote that we are good and worthy, rather than fat, worthless, and lazy, or whatever the learned criticism might be. The myth of singularity tells us that we will be healthy when we stop having negative thoughts about ourselves. A more real-world approach tells us that we are being healthy when we refuse to participate in the perpetual abuse cycle within our own consciousness.

Sam discovered that, when challenged to make his condemning messages directly to his inner child, he could not do it. In later sessions, he was able to be compassionate and even complimentary and supportive toward the child. Some people, however, are able to speak the critical, condemning messages to their inner child in this exercise. The good news about that is when light is shone on the reality of such inner abuse, the person's tolerance for the abuse is reduced over time. The more real the relationship between adult and inner child, the lower the tolerance for mistreatment and the stronger the desire to support and love the child.

It didn't take long to realize that the only reason to discover an inner child was to motivate the development of an inner parent to take care of that child. Many of us have already spent years feeling like children lost in a world of adults. We need to learn how to step up to the plate as fully functioning adults. Ironically, we will finally be able to do that once we identify the vulnerable child within us. There is nothing particularly complicated about this. Quite simply, as long as you identify yourself as the adult responsible for the child, you are not being the child. Within our multiple consciousness, several aspects of our personalities exist simultaneously, but identity cannot occupy two places at the same time. Only from the perspective of being the adult can you do what it takes to protect and nurture your inner child.

Even if you have previously thought of the inner-child metaphor as namby-pamby psychobabble, I hope you will give this a try. Find a photograph or two of yourself as a child. Put one in a frame and keep it visible in your home or office. No one else has to know that you are having a relationship with a photo. Practice saying—verbally or silently—kind, loving things to the image of yourself as a child. And the next time you are being especially critical of yourself, take "Sam's challenge" and imagine your negative inner chatter aimed directly at the child in the picture frame. By doing this, you will offer yourself a choice about how to treat yourself, a choice that you may not have previously known you had.

We all have the capacity and the responsibility to make our own choices. This is another of the simple truths that we must be careful not to rush by. It is all too easy to say, "Of course, of course, I know that," without considering the full implications. We say that we know that the choices are ours to make, but frequently our thoughts and behaviors are not congruent with these words. Consider how often we use, and hear, statements like, "I had no choice," or "There was only one thing I could do," or "I was forced to do what I did."

An alcoholic client early in recovery says to me, "I know that I cannot drink because I am an alcoholic." At first glance, this appears to be a statement of responsibility, but I think it is not. At the very least, it is not enough. It is certainly a positive statement for an alcoholic to say, but it stops short of accepting full responsibility.

I explain to my client how I differ on this point and why it is important. "I am an alcoholic," I tell him, "and I can drink." I pause because I know that hearing this sentence coming from his recovering alcoholic therapist will confuse him. Momentary confusion is sometimes an excellent tool for getting someone's full attention. "I have proven all too well," I continue, "that I can drink. I can drink mine and several other people's shares. What I cannot do is drink alcohol and expect a positive outcome. I have proven that I can drink, and I have proven that the results will sooner or later (usually sooner) be extremely negative. So, I increase the accuracy of the statement by saying 'I am an alcoholic and I cannot drink without creating problems for myself,' and I can increase the power of the statement by saying, 'I am an alcoholic, so I won't drink.'"

I have been accused of needlessly picking at the semantics on this point, but I disagree with that criticism. The simple switch of "won't" for "can't" makes a tremendous difference when it comes to accepting full responsibility for our choices. "Won't" is an expression of choice, implying that we are in charge, while "can't" implies that we either have no choice or are incapable of making a choice. Distinguishing "won't" from "can't" is integral in understanding that we can either watch our lives go by or jump in and become the playmakers.

When Sam was instructed to voice his criticism aloud to his inner child, he said "I can't." I understood that in that moment he literally could not bring himself to insult the little boy made tangible by the exercise. And in that moment, I would have only been distracting him from the important emotional experience if I attempted to explain the difference between "can't" and "won't." But the truth is Sam was capable of criticizing his inner child. The difficulty he encountered was in his own value system. Sam is a person who would not knowingly speak abusively to a child. Sam was not incapable of insulting his inner child. What happened that day, as I later explained to him, was more about the capacity of his personal value system than it was his incapacity to be hurtful and negative. Sam could insult his inner child. After all, he had been doing it for years. But once the experience was brought into the light and seen for what it was, the fully capable adult Sam refused to contribute to the abuse.

Because I am an alcoholic, with a proven track record demonstrating my capacity and tendency to drink alcohol with devastating results, I won't take a drink today. I refuse to do it. Is there something you need to refuse to do?

Essentially what I have learned about this, what I continue to learn, and what I teach others is how to stop being life's victim, how to identify ourselves as the ones in charge—even if not in control—of the lives we lead. A simple clarification of definition helps here (another Nutshell): victims believe how they are doing is determined by what happens to them; nonvictims believe how they are doing is determined by how they respond to what happens to them. There is a tremendous difference between these two perspectives.

We remain in charge of our lives even when we are not in control. To be in charge simply means that we accept that we alone are responsible for making the decisions about what to do or not do with the circumstances (the cards) dealt us. I may say that I have no choice but to pay my bills every month, but of course that is not so. Although I do not control the mortgage company, the electric company, the water department, and so on, it is up to me how I will respond to the bills they send.

To recognize that we have a choice in all situations does not have a thing to do with whether or not we are in control of those situations. Remember the definition for wisdom: the growing lists of what we do not control and what we do not know. In the midst of these ever increasing lists, we maintain authority over our lives, whether we like it or not, whether we admit it or not, and even whether we recognize it or not. We don't really have any choice in the matter.

Another of the simple truths I have come to accept is that *resistance to change is natural.* In the psychotherapy business, much is made of "dealing with resistance," especially when treating addictive disorders. But I think that as clinicians, we do more harm than good when we characterize a client as "resistant," "not motivated," or "noncompliant." What possible good could come from my pitting myself against a client, ready to argue her into a state of mental health? The answer to that question may seem obvious, but I have seen this approach not only practiced, but celebrated as highly effective. It is really nothing more than a form of brainwashing. When it does work—when a client has been bullied into thinking the "right way"—the success lacks the depth necessary for genuine, lasting change, because the client has not so much taken charge of his own life, as he has just handed authority over to another person or system of thought.

Fear lies beneath resistance and when we insist on constant cooperation from others or ourselves, we will almost certainly be rushing prematurely—and therefore inadequately—through our acronym map. Ultimately, overcompliance accomplishes the same thing as classic resistance: the avoidance of being in the scary middle ground characterized by uncertainty.

I once worked with a young man, Jeff, who had completed three well-respected residential alcohol- and drug-dependency treatment programs in a span of seven or eight years. Jeff came to see me because he was still not able to abstain from alcohol for more than two weeks at a time. As I spoke with him about what had and had not been helpful in these previous treatments, I discovered that none of his counselors encouraged him to explore his own thinking about the diagnosis of alcoholism. Jeff's thinking, one counselor told him, was "sick" and therefore needed to be ignored. Summary reports from the treatment programs confirmed my suspicion that he had been perceived as resistant and "uncooperative" in each of the programs. The treatment plans had been developed to "break through" Jeff's denial, but I could see no evidence of anyone helping Jeff to face his own internal struggle about alcohol use. As is too often the case, Jeff's resistance was seen by each of the treatment programs' staff as the enemy, an aspect of Jeff's thinking that had to be destroyed in order for him to get well.

I was fortunate early in my career to hear the psychologist and author Richard Bandler say, "There is no such thing as resistant clients; there are only inflexible therapists." These days I repeat Dr. Bandler's line whenever I am speaking to a group of my peers and colleagues. It is an excellent reminder of our responsibility as clinicians: our job is to help people change, not just explain why they don't.

Resistance is the natural and logical result of our multiple nature. In our external environments, at work for instance, we may form a committee so that various perspectives and opinions can be represented. As long as there is an accepted system for making decisions, the diversity of such a committee is a strength. The same is true for our inner committees. Believe it or not, struggle among your committee members is not only natural, it can be extremely productive.

Rather than thinking of resistance as part of the problem, think of it as a part of the process of finding a solution. We are more likely to become bogged down in problems when we fail to acknowledge the variety of opinions and feelings within the one mind. Let all your committee members have their say and think of yourself as the Decision

Maker, sitting at the head of the conference-room table. Everyone gets to speak, but only you get to decide what you will do.

In other words, be the Decision Maker, and expect—even embrace—your own resistance. Another Nutshell posted in my office reads: "I reserve the right to disagree with myself." I exercise that right frequently, and I encourage you to do the same.

It is helpful and can even be fun to draw a diagram of your committee. In my image the Decision Maker is standing, not sitting, at the head of a long conference-room table, with the various committee members lining both sides. One of my clients sees her committee in a big circle with her Decision Maker in the center sitting in a swivel chair with rollers. Use your imagination and find the most helpful depiction of your committee. Identify as many members of the committee as you can, but don't worry too much about that. As you think in terms of multiplicity, you will recognize more and more of the committee members. Identify and even name them as you become aware of them. This may seem silly, but it really is a more accurate depiction of our mind than the one propagated by the myth of singularity.

As you change your relationship with fear and as you meet your committee, expect to hear the voice of resistance. It will tell you that the NO FEAR motto is stupid, climbing down the ladder is ridiculous, and our acronym map will never work. Acknowledge the voice of resistance and realize that it is just one committee member's point of view. Only the Decision Maker determines whether or not you will face and overcome fear's control. By understanding that resistance is natural, we remind ourselves that we are not going through this alone. We can reach out and remind each other that no matter how rocky the road, both the journey and the destination are well worth the bumps.

After acknowledging responsibility for choosing the paths we take and recognizing the existence and even the value of natural resistance, we come to another of the simple truths we all have in common: *willingness, not willpower, is the key to sustaining personal growth.* Willpower is closed and rigid; willingness is open and flexible. Willpower connotes a sort of "John Wayne" self-reliance, while willingness remains open to every resource available. Many people who seek psychotherapy express a sense of shame based on a belief that needing therapy indicates weakness. The opposite is closer to the truth. It takes a lot more guts to admit the need for help and show up for therapy than it does to hide our heads in the sand, pretending to have no problems. Ultimately, to be willing is a much stronger position than to possess incredible willpower. The Nutshell reads: "Measure strength according to willingness instead of willpower."

One of the first clients I saw when I began my psychotherapy practice many years ago was a well-dressed real-estate agent named Ben.

"This is going to be easy," I thought, as he began telling me why he had made the appointment.

"There's no doubt about it," Ben said. "I have a cocaine

problem." His wife had confronted him about his late nights and neglect of the family and insisted he get some help. "But I'm not here for her," Ben explained. "I'm here for me. I want help. I'm willing to do whatever I need to do to beat this thing."

Ben had already given me enough of a history of his alcohol and drug use for me to know that he was into addiction pretty deep. When I heard him say the magic word "willing," that's when I began thinking this was going to be an easy day's work.

"I'm glad to hear that," I told Ben when he had said that he was willing to do whatever he needed to do. "I am going to recommend that you admit yourself to Cumberland Heights. It's an excellent addiction treatment center located just outside of town. I'm going to give you this phone number, and . . . "

"Wait, wait, wait," Ben jumped in. "I don't want to go into a treatment program."

"But I thought you said you were willing to do whatever was necessary," I reminded him.

"I am. But not that. I don't want to go into a treatment program. I am willing to do anything else, though."

Again I heard the word "willing," so I offered an alternative plan. "Okay, we can develop an outpatient treatment plan for you. I'll need to see you here for individual sessions a couple of times each week, and I want you to attend Alcoholics Anonymous and Cocaine Anonymous meetings every day."

"Hold on there," Ben started again. "I don't think I need to go to those meetings. I'm not an alcoholic . . . "

"Ben, you really would be better off in the program at Cumberland Heights." It was my turn to interrupt. "And since you are not willing to do that, I really believe that you need to be in a support meeting at least one time per day."

"Well, I don't have time to do that, even if that is what I need. I have a business to run."

"Okay," I said, a little discouraged. It didn't occur to me to ask him how he had been consistently able to make so much time for substance abuse for the past several years. "What are you willing to do?"

Ben brightened right up. "Anything," he said, with no irony intended. "Like I told you, I want to lick this thing. Besides going to that treatment program or those daily meetings, I'm willing to follow your lead. You tell me."

"All right," I said. "Let's schedule some sessions for you here, and I want you to also attend an addiction education group that meets once a week . . . "

"Whoa there, partner," Ben said, putting the brakes on once more. "How about I just come to see you a couple more times. I like you. You seem like you know what you're doing. I think with your help, I can beat this thing."

These many years later, I have had countless conversations with clients who were every bit as "willing" to do whatever it takes as Ben was. The fact is Ben had come face to face with a major wall in his life, and other than getting his wife off his back, he did not have the slightest inclination to do anything about it. He was, at least for that moment, willing to continue to run headlong into his wall and pretend that it wasn't there. Ben's lack of willingness left him about six miles short of even the first letter of our acronym map.

Not surprisingly, I never heard from Ben again after that initial meeting. Was Ben one of those resistant clients who Richard Bandler says doesn't exist? You bet he was. But more important, I was one of those inflexible (and quite naive) therapists. My one-track strategy was to bypass Ben's resistance to getting the help he needed, even though facing his resistance was what he needed the help for. My approach to Ben in that session was analogous to the driving instructor who insists that you drive yourself to his office to make arrangements for your first lesson, or the oncologist who says that he will begin chemotherapy as soon as your cancer moves into remission.

It could be said that Ben had a strong will, but lacked the willingness to do what it would take to recover from his chemical addiction. Willingness, after all, is essential to bringing about genuine change. I find it more productive to consider that I failed to recognize his willingness to show up at all as the potential beginning for our work together. No matter how sound my recommendations for treatment might have been, trying to impose them on him in that first session was the well-intentioned imposition of my will onto Ben. We were both experiencing problems with willingness that day.

Last week, fifteen years after my meeting with Ben, I met with a young woman named Lori whose husband suspects she might have the eating disorder, bulimia. Like Ben, she told me that she was there for herself, but acknowledged that her husband had been instrumental in her making the appointment. As we began getting to know each other, I spent most of my time listening to her, rather than making my immediate recommendations, as I had with Ben. I was curious about what Lori wanted; I wondered how fear was getting in her way.

Ben was barely aware of his wall of resistance when I had shone a spotlight on it and pushed him toward it. He responded by running the other way. Lori has made it as far as my office, and I am determined to sit with her as she decides what she will do.

I will listen, curious to discover how a few simple truths might be working—or not working—in Lori's life. I expect that she and I will discover the distinctive voice of resistance on her committee and work toward empowering her Decision Maker. But I won't rush her down the path, my own enthusiasm shouting, "Hurry, hurry, come on. You're going to love this." This is not my path; it is hers. Just as your path is not mine; it is yours.

Each of us must choose for ourselves not only what we are willing to do, but also when we are willing to do it. Lori will choose when to take necessary steps toward her wall. And so will you.

CHAPTER EIGHT

Up Against the Wall
When It's Time to Challenge Fear

God will not have his work manifest by cowards.
—RALPH WALDO EMERSON

FOR AS LONG AS I CAN REMEMBER, I planned on being a writer. By the time I was in college, a drunken English major, my plans had evolved into the completely unrealistic belief that I was so talented (undiscovered and underappreciated) that I was sure to become quite successful as a poet. (I was not familiar with the word "oxymoron" when I was thinking I was destined to become a successful poet.) Never mind that I seldom submitted anything for publication, and when I did, it was either a short poem to the college literary magazine or a collected mess of poetry about girls who would not go out with me sent to one of the large publishing houses. I did not have a clue about the work I would need to do if I were to have even the slightest chance of being published at all. I honestly believed that fame and fortune would find me.

When I finally realized that fame and fortune were not even looking for me, I decided to change my major to psychology. I based this decision largely on two considerations. First, I had made an A in Introductory Psychology my freshman year and, second, I would not have to take any classes at eight o'clock in the morning. I really didn't think it past that point. Looking back, I realize that I was much too busy working on my true major: avoiding the challenges of life at all costs. Regardless of what my transcript will tell you, that is the major I successfully completed.

As a psychotherapist, I have heard so many similar stories—some more, some less extreme than mine—I have given it a name. I call it "living by default." When we live by default, we are sleepwalking, inadvertently (of course) devoted to taking the paths of least resistance. When we walk up to or bump into a fear, we simply turn and walk in another direction or veer off to one side or the other. People choose careers this way, enter marriages this way, and develop value systems this way. Some people never awaken from this sleep state. They live asleep, and they die asleep. Others of us are awakened by one kind of disturbance or another, and if we are fortunate enough to not fall back to sleep, we find ourselves somewhere in an adult's body, somewhere in an adult's life, trying to figure out how we got here and, more important, facing the challenge of what to do about it.

If you have lived your life by default and would now like to wake up, you must make a commitment to live your new

life—that is, the life that always begins right now—by decision. You cannot choose your major according to what time
the classes meet, and you cannot afford to believe that
whatever success you desire is out there somewhere looking
for you. You have picked up this book as surely as I have
written it. We both face the challenge of living our lives by
decision rather than default. Sometimes this will feel exhil-
arating, and at other times we will wish with all our minds
and hearts that we could drift back to sleep. And sometimes
we do.

I have a friend who seems fearless in the face of decision,
even big, ominous, important decisions. He doesn't say he's
fearless, only that he is "not particularly influenced" by fear.
I am not like that, and neither are most of the people I have
spoken with through the years. Fortunately, those of us who
are afraid and who are "frequently influenced" by our fear
are the norm. We are not alone. That is always good news.

Recently in a workshop about the connection between
self-compassion and personal responsibility, I asked participants to talk about the frightening prospect of living lives by
decision rather than default. Even when we can all agree
that living by decision is a far more attractive option, the
internal resistance remains. In many cases, making a commitment to live by decision actually increases the activity of
resistance. One workshop participant gave an excellent
example of this: "I am the consummate self-saboteur. You
can bet that literally within twenty-four hours of my making
an important decision, I will begin the downhill slide. First,
self-doubt consumes me. 'Who do I think I am? What makes

me think I can do this or that?' Then my energy drains. Whatever enthusiasm I had for whatever I had decided is simply gone. And I am left wondering what I ever saw in the idea in the first place."

Another participant added: "I know what you mean about the energy drain. But the way I sabotage myself is by immediately sharing my ideas with friends and family, who will predictably shoot me down. So I guess my resistance to living by decision makes use of outside consultants."

Such self-sabotage is fueled by fear, but fortunately we don't have to be rid of that fuel source in order to defeat our resistance. We simply have to put our acronym map to work: become aware of the fear and accept it as part of the experience. *Acceptance* that fear is here whether we like it or not is an essential step in cutting the fuel line. Remember our simple truth: resistance is a natural part of the process. Our challenge is to pay attention and continue learning from the resistance. And fortunately, the goal is not to live without fear, but to live a life not ruled by fear. Be positive and be realistic.

Often when I suggest to clients that they "accept" their fear, they mistakenly think that I am telling them that they should "agree with" their fear. Not so. Becoming aware of something and accepting that it exists have nothing to do with forming an opinion one way or another about it. For instance, I accept that my eyesight is far less than 20/20, and I demonstrate that acceptance every morning when I put on my eyeglasses. I also accept the fact that I know how to listen to people and respond in particular ways that are helpful. I demonstrate that acceptance when I go to the office to see clients. These are two very different truths, and I accept them both.

The fear that fuels our resistance is neither a good thing nor a bad thing. It simply is. Experiencing fear is a normal part of being a living, breathing creature. When we invest our time and energy into attempts to rid ourselves of fear, we are wasting that time and energy. The challenge that comes with living by decision rather than default is to become familiar with our fear. You may think you already know your fear, but there is an important difference between knowing your fear and being ruled by it. Just because it controls you doesn't mean you know it. To get to know your fear, you must learn to stand in its presence. Practice standing in the presence of fear, doing absolutely nothing more than being aware and awake.

In the workshop, we begin the afternoon session with a visualization called "The Wall." It is an exercise in guided imagery to help make tangible the experience of standing in the presence of resistance and fear. I include it here, along with suggestions about how you might put the imagery to work for yourself and, later, some responses from workshop participants.

The Wall

Imagine yourself standing in front of a big brick wall. Just you and the wall. How close do you stand? And what do you feel when you are facing the wall?

How wide is your wall? And how high? Can you see where the wall ends? Where it begins? Can you reach the top?

How old is the wall—or how new? Who built it? And why? How long have you been here? Are you alone? How long do you plan to stay?

It's your wall, you know. Touch it. Feel its texture. Feel whatever you feel.

What is on the other side of the wall? Can you guess? Do you know? Have you ever been there? Do you want to go there now?

What if you are not alone? What if there is more here than just you and the wall? What if we are there with you?

What if you are wrong about the strength of the wall? What if you are wrong about your own potential? You've been wrong before, haven't you?

Your wall is made of bricks—individual bricks. The wall is big. The bricks are small. The mortar is of your own making. How strong is it?

What if you destroy your wall? What if you destroy your wall, and then regret it? What if you miss it? What if you can't handle it on the other side of the wall? What if it's too late to turn back now?

Now put your hand on your wall. Touch it, palm flat on the wall. What happens? Push. What happens? Both hands. What happens?

Will you step through? Do you dare? Can you keep yourself from it? Can you let yourself stumble, and laugh when you fall through to the other side of . . . ? What's left of the wall?

What is it like on this side of the wall? The sky, the ground, the air around you—what is it like? What do you see? What do you hear? And what do you feel?

And what's that in the distance?

The visualization itself is quite simple. My wife calls it a subjective mini-movie. In brief, you face a wall, become aware, touch the wall, push through the wall, and step through—or fall through—to the other side. What could be simpler? What's the big deal?

The big deal, I have discovered, is that everyone has a wall—at least one. The big deal is that the wall is a simple and clear metaphor for whatever ails us. I have also discovered that the wall is not, as we tend to assume, an obstacle between me and the life I want to live. To think in these terms encourages an attitude of postponement—that is, I will begin as soon as this or that happens, or as soon as I overcome this or that obstacle, or as soon as I accomplish this or that goal. With this thinking we are in danger of spending years, even decades, waiting to begin. It is wise to consider the work of facing our walls as the essence of life, rather than a distraction from life.

The language of "The Wall" is a series of questions. The questions are what will put you into the mini-movie, making it a subjective experience. It is important to remember the Nutshell on my wall that reads: "Forget about finding the right answers; just make a list of some very good questions."

Good questions are powerful. Like magnets, they attract information to us. I listen for the questions that my clients might be asking without knowing it. And when, in the collaborative spirit of the therapy, we have mined out a good question or two, I recommend that my client write them down and carry them in a pocket or tape them on the car dashboard. "Let the question do its work," I say. "Let each good question attract many answers." There can never be too many answers. Every answer a question attracts is information we can use.

I encourage you to do the same. Maybe even designate a good question section in your journal or keep a separate little notebook called *Good Questions*.

Listen for the rhetorical questions we tend to ask ourselves, the questions that are actually thinly veiled insults. Questions such as "What's wrong with me?" "Why can't I ever get this right?" or "Why don't I just give up?" can be transformed into powerful tools when we decide to take the questions at face value and use them as magnets to attract useful information. In the past, when I asked the question "What's wrong with me?" the answer was implied: everything is wrong with me; I am hopeless. When clients insult themselves with rhetorical questions, I push the pause button and suggest that we put the real question to work for us. Do that with your list of questions. Listen past the insult and allow each question to do its work.

If I am experiencing frustration or fear as a public speaker, and my inner critic asks, "What's wrong with you?" I might take the question away from the inner critic and ask it as a real question. A real question is one asked with genuine curiosity, for the purpose of gathering information I may not already have. So I ask, "What is wrong with me?" and collect the following answers with my magnet:

I am tired and have not been sleeping well.

I am lapsing back into my perfectionism, thinking that everything I say must be profound and perfect for every person in my audience.

I am forgetting that I feel much better, more confident, when I schedule time to rehearse my presentations.

I am unrealistically critical of myself and have a tendency to avoid what scares me.

Quite simply, I am scared that what I have to say will not be good enough.

The question itself can continue to collect answers, and the answers will vary from hour to hour, day to day, and week to week. But with just these few answers attracted by the question, you can see how I already have more specific information to put toward solving my problem. Usually, the more times we ask the question, the deeper the answers will go. In the example above, the information revealed by my answers begins with a lack of sleep and ends with a direct expression of fear. If that sounds familiar, it is because we are climbing down the ladder again, continually looking deeper and deeper. The deeper the information, the more profound the subsequent change will be.

The questions that make up "The Wall" are asked with genuine curiosity. Make the curiosity your own. If you would like to do the wall visualization, find a comfortable place to sit or lie down and ask a friend to read it to you. Ask your friend to read through it a time or two first, to become familiar with it, then to read it slowly while you close your eyes, relax a little, and experience whatever you experience. Or you can record your own voice reading "The Wall" and play the tape back for yourself.

Just as there are many answers to any one good question, your experience with the visualization will probably vary each time you use it. If you are feeling stuck in your life, your experience may vary only a little, but I encourage you to pay close attention to even the most minor differences. Change usually comes in small increments. You can't actually see a child growing, but you can certainly recognize the growth. And when in doubt, I always remember Bill Murray's wonderful character in the movie *What About Bob?* "Baby steps," Bob Wiley reminds us. "Baby steps to the elevator." Baby steps to the wall. Baby steps beyond the wall.

Following the guided visualization, I ask participants to respond first to only the beginning of "The Wall," representing that point in time when we awaken to the very real presence of our fear and the resistance that it fuels. I ask participants to close their eyes again, as I remind them of the first few lines: "Imagine yourself standing in front of a big brick wall. Just you and the wall. How close do you stand? And what do you feel when you are facing the wall?" Here are some of the responses from a recent workshop. One person said: "I could feel the fear in my entire body as I stood facing my wall. The fear told me to run, or crumble, or hide, to do anything but stand there. I couldn't take my eyes off the wall in front of me. And it took everything in me to just stand there, doing nothing."

Another participant picked up the ball: "I didn't just stand there. I guess I ran away, because my mind just drifted off into other thoughts. A couple of times I remembered I was supposed to be standing in front of some wall, but then my mind would just wander off again. I wasn't aware of any fear."

We talked for a moment about how the absence of fear probably meant that the psychological defenses (a wandering mind, in this case) were working effectively.

Another participant spoke: "I didn't feel so much afraid as mad. I was angry. I guess I was offended by the wall. I was inundated by 'should's.' I shouldn't have a wall, or I should be able to just push it over, or just walk straight through it. Now that I think about it, I was mostly angry with myself— like I was some kind of big disappointment."

As is often the case, we soon discovered that "feeling like some kind of disappointment" was a troublesome recurring life theme for this participant.

One participant reported feeling empowered from the very start: "This was very vivid for me. I spread my feet shoulder width in the visualization, taking a physical stance that I associate with power. I stood there just like you told us, and I felt the fear. It was like I was even inviting the fear in. I didn't feel it so much in my body as it was like it was all around me, washing over me. But I just stood there. I felt strangely calm. I kept thinking, 'I'm okay. Whatever this is, it can't hurt me if I don't let it.' This was very strange for me because usually it is impossible for me to stand still for more than a couple of seconds."

The challenge in the beginning of the visualization is to remain still, to let simple awareness work for you. Awareness is highly underestimated as an agent of change, when in fact it is the vehicle that carries us through our acronym map. Too often we are inclined to take action so quickly that we are pulled prematurely away from becoming aware of the truth around us. When you first awaken, when you open your eyes to discover the wall in front of you, remember that awareness is your most precious instrument, your direct link to the practical information you need to navigate success-fully through life. Wait out the temptation to take immediate action. Don't turn and run, don't crumble, and don't close your eyes again. Neither retreat, nor aggress. Take no action against the wall. Simply stand there, inviting awareness to teach you.

Carly, the workshop participant haunted by the "I'm some kind of disappointment" message, joined one of my weekly therapy groups shortly after the workshop. In the few weeks we have worked together now, she has already made excellent use of the wall metaphor in helping her to not only squarely face her fears, but also begin to push through those fears, moving in the direction of some very specific goals.

For a while, Carly's "disappointment theme" continued to successfully rob her of whatever power she had built up to face the wall. "I get to feeling better, really fired up about taking charge of my life," she said, "and then it feels like the bottom just drops out from under me. I end up right where I started: not able to make the easiest of decisions. When I'm like that, I couldn't tell you for sure what dressing I want on my salad."

Then, with the growing support of other group members telling her that she is not a disappointment, Carly learned to prepare for the predictable, negative messages that in the past triggered the bottom to drop out. She learned to visualize the negative messages associated with the bottom dropping out as members of her committee, standing around her as she faced the wall. The important part of this was that Carly was becoming able to perceive herself as separate and distinct from the negative messages. She added the other group members and a couple of her most supportive friends to her visualization.

Here is how Carly described it: "Now I am standing about an arm's distance from the wall, and there are many people around me. The supportive ones and the negative ones are all mingling together. I am aware of both, very different kinds of energy, but all there in this one place, at this one time."

"Do you feel influenced more by one or the other, the positive or the negative?" I asked.

"This may seem bizarre, but the two energies seem kind of balanced. I am aware of both, and it feels like either one could step forward and become the dominant energy."

This was a very positive description in and of itself, because Carly had originally felt very alone, without support, as she faced her wall.

"Can you ask the positive supportive people to step forward to reinforce their connection to you?" I asked.

Carly's response was immediate. "It's done. Just as you were saying that, you guys [referring to those of us in the group, plus her two friends] moved toward me, away from the crowd. You have formed a semicircle behind me, and I can feel our collective power building in front of the wall." She paused, then smiled. "This feels good. I am definitely not alone this time."

Since Carly has become so attached to the wall visualization, in the coming weeks I am sure the group will return to the wall with her. We may explore its dimensions, its history and origins, its feel, its texture. We may explore Carly's beliefs about her wall and what she imagines is on the other side. We may—as often is the case—reflect on her hesitation to push through the wall. "What if you destroy the wall, and then regret it?" the visualization asks. And we will probably witness Carly pushing through the wall, her falling through to the other side. What will all this mean for Carly? How will it impact the other members of the group? Time will tell.

"The Wall" evokes many different responses in us, but the one that I hear people talking about most often is the experience of feeling overwhelmed. This is only natural because a decision to face your wall delivers you directly to the need for another decision: the decision to do whatever it will take to conquer the wall. This decision is impossible to make without a certain amount of faith—or maybe delusion. (To explore the difference between the two, I suggest you read *Don Quixote*.) We understandably wonder, "How can I decide to do something when I am not sure what it will take?" or "Will I be up to the task?" We want to know what is possible before we make our commitment. We live in a world characterized by uncertainty, and yet we demand to be certain before proceeding. The relevant Nutshell reads: "I think uncertainty is the nature of life . . . but I can't be sure."

As you stand facing your wall, I urge you to become fully aware of your fears, and I challenge you to let go of your need for certainty. When you ask, "How can I know that I can do this?" the answer will return, "You cannot know the outcome in advance, but you absolutely can know that you have the power and the authority to take the action."

You cannot know the results of your efforts in advance, but it can be helpful to think back, remembering something else you learned that at first overwhelmed you and seemed impossible. Think, for instance, of learning to drive a standard-shift car or how to play a musical instrument. Or think of the baby who decides it is time to walk. How many times do you grind the gears or miss the note and how many times does the baby fall before the goal is attained?

The baby is the best role model here. How many times will the baby fall before he walks? The answer: as many times as it takes. When is the last time you saw a grown man crawling on hands and knees because as a baby he became so frustrated with learning to walk that he gave up trying?

I hope you will revisit "The Wall" several times as you continue to read this book. I have never found anyone who reports having the exact same experience twice. There are always changes, even if one is an increase in your frustration as you run headfirst into the bricks one more time. You may also experience more drastic changes. I remember one workshop participant who described his surprise when, during a third visit to the wall, he discovered a jackhammer in his hands. Another woman spontaneously passed through her wall without disturbing the structure in the least. The key is to experience whatever you experience, to let go as much as you can of any preconceived expectations you have for yourself or that you believe others may have for you.

It's your wall, after all.

CHAPTER NINE

The Push
Leaning into the Fear

Nothing is so much to be feared as fear.
—HENRY DAVID THOREAU

YOUR WALL IS MADE OF BRICKS—individual bricks. The wall is big. The bricks are small. The mortar is of your own making. How strong is it? This is my favorite part of "The Wall" visualization. To me, it says simply this: the bricks are not the problem—the mortar is. And the mortar is made of—you guessed it—fear.

My client Jenni insisted on knowing what the bricks represent in the visualization. "Fear is the mortar; I understand that. But what are the bricks?"

Once more the collaboration of the therapy process was at work. After a couple of conversations on the subject, it was ultimately Jenni who answered her own question—to my benefit and now to yours.

"The bricks are life itself," Jenni explained. "Each brick represents a different aspect of life, and some bricks are very specific events."

"Do you mind if I write this down?" I asked her. I could tell she was making an important contribution to understanding, and therefore benefiting from, the wall metaphor.

"The bricks generally represent things like job, marriage, school, economic status, health, and other relationships with parents, children, friends, and co-workers. If you look closer at a wall at a particular time in someone's life, the bricks represent more specific circumstances—like a particular relationship, a specific event at work or home, a test at school, a Thanksgiving holiday with family, a health problem, a social event. On a broader scale, bricks can represent a wide range of things, including concerns about civil rights, education for children, and global terrorism.

"Do you see? The bricks are just life's component parts. They come in all sizes—small, medium, and large. As individuals, we don't generally choose our bricks. To mix this with one of your favorite metaphors, these are just the cards—in this case, bricks—that are dealt us." Jenni pointed to one of the Nutshells on the wall: "Be in charge of your life. Forget about being in control."

"So even though I can't change the essence of the brick itself, I am in charge of what I choose to do with my bricks," I said. "I can build something useful, or not. It's my choice."

"Right," Jenni said.

"And when we use fear as mortar, the result is a big solid wall of our own making," I added.

Jenni summed it up: "With fear, we create walls out of life itself."

Think about it. If we weaken the mortar, if we interfere with the stability of this fear-based substance, the bricks in the wall pose not much more of an obstacle than a house of cards. Weaken the mortar—destroy the fear—and then push. What happens? Return to the visualization to see and feel this. Imagine that you have contaminated the mortar, rendering it extremely porous and brittle. Place your palms against the wall and push. See what happens. And feel what happens within you when you do this. And ask yourself, "What will I choose to build with my bricks?" This time, instead of using fear as your mortar, use our acronym map— FEAR: *face the fear; explore it; accept it;* and *respond to it.* These four steps, designed to transform your relationship with fear, will make the difference between a life well lived and a big brick wall.

But let's not get ahead of ourselves. The first question here is where we find a contaminate for our mortar. How do we weaken the fears? The answer is that we move directly toward them. The strongest fears are the unexamined fears. Like vampires, our fears do not fare well in the bright light of day. Another Nutshell on my office wall reads: "Always move toward your demons; they take their power from your retreat."

I demonstrate this with clients and workshop participants from time to time. I sit face to face with a person, and ask that she lean forward in her chair. "Lean toward me," I say, "as if you are in charge of me, as if you are imposing your authority on me." In turn, I lean as far back into my chair as I can, in retreat, basically abdicating my authority, handing my power over to my partner in this exercise. I did this the other day in a workshop with a woman named Dorothy. As I did my best to melt into the back of my chair, I asked Dorothy to describe her experience.

"It's kind of uncomfortable, probably because it seems so foreign to me, but mostly I feel powerful," Dorothy said.

I asked her, "Right here, right now, who is in charge?"

"I am," Dorothy said.

Next I had Dorothy, in her forward-leaning position, take on the role of a negative, fear-based member of my inner committee. At this point in the exercise, you will see that I leave the negative messages rather general, so that as many people can identify as possible. I'll tell you what I tell workshop participants: feel free to plug in your more specific negative self-talk. I reminded Dorothy to remain "in charge" by holding her physical position of leaning toward me, instructing her to read from an index card I handed her: "Thom, you are pitiful. There is no way you will succeed, no matter what you say or what you do. The only thing you will succeed at is making a fool of yourself. You are a loser. You have always been and always will be a loser. Give it up. The only chance you have is keeping a low profile. If you're lucky, maybe people won't notice you."

After Dorothy had read the card to me twice, I sat quietly for a few moments, allowing everyone in the room to experience the heavy feeling that seems to literally hang in the air in the wake of such negative, condemning statements.

Then I asked her again, "Who is in charge here?"

"I am." Dorothy's reply was instantaneous. And she said it with an authority that I think surprised even her. As is usually the case with this exercise, Dorothy could feel the power that came with her position.

"You are in charge. That's right. Do you know why? What about our little experiment puts you in charge?"

"I suppose it is my body language, and the negative things I said to you. I am in charge because I am sitting up, leaning forward, and criticizing you," Dorothy said with increasing confidence.

Abruptly I sat forward, moved to the very edge of my chair, interlaced my fingers, and put my forearms on my knees. I had moved suddenly to a face-to-face position with Dorothy, my nose no more than six inches from hers. "Wrong," I said. "What put you in charge before was not your leaning forward; it was my leaning back. And now," I said with deliberate sternness, "you are no longer in charge, are you?"

Dorothy was silent, and then with a not so powerful voice she said, "No."

The response to this exercise is always fun, because the person in Dorothy's seat is not the only one who experiences it. I asked the other participants what they saw, thought, and felt. The responses in this workshop were similar to responses every time I do this.

"I felt surprised," said one young man, "almost like I was sitting in Dorothy's place."

Someone else said, "The change was dramatic. Thom, it was as if you appeared out of nowhere. You just materialized in Dorothy's face."

Dorothy said, "My response was very physical. My chest tightened up. And I don't know if I literally moved back, but inside I know that is exactly what I did."

To Dorothy, someone observed, "You didn't back up, but you flinched. And after the flinch, you were no longer in charge."

What I always hope to demonstrate with this exercise is that no matter what the inner criticism, threat, or prophecy, we do not have to change it. I have wasted far too much time in my life—and watched others do the same—trying to get rid of negative, fear-based thoughts and beliefs. I may be a broken record on this point, but it is extremely important: *we do not have to get rid of anything.* No matter how troubling, frightening, or annoying the message emanating from within us, *all we have to do is perceive ourselves as separate from that toxic message and disagree with it.* And even when disagreement seems too much to ask, we can still disobey. For instance, when my negative inner message implies that I should avoid taking action by telling me that I am "destined to fail" or "bound to make a fool of myself," my best bet is to plow ahead, fear and all, refusing to be slowed or paralyzed by my well-rehearsed inner terrorism. "Thank you for sharing," I say to this fear-based, avoidance advocate on my committee. "Now please take your seat."

I am not suggesting that this is easy to do. Like learning anything else, we must find the specific techniques and then practice them. You should not expect yourself to change your inner relationship dynamics without a willingness to practice, practice, practice, anymore than I should expect to play the piano after a couple of lessons.

Following my demonstration with Dorothy, the other participants were invited to pair off and experiment with leaning one way and then another. What is discovered is that the balance of power in this little exercise is not determined by the size of the person or the person's gender, unless a participant has had a historically significant experience with one gender or the other. For instance, a person with a domineering father might find it more difficult to lean forward in the exercise if his partner is male. The balance of power is determined by the position we take in response to the message. Just as in our external relationships, it is always more powerful to stand up for ourselves, rather than against someone else.

When we take our stand believing that the mission is to defeat or destroy the Bully, we make the mistake of standing against something. When we move toward the fear, understanding that the fear does not need to change as long as we are willing to change our relationship to it, we stand up for ourselves. If you can enjoy a scary movie, rent a movie called *House,* starring William Katt, George Wendt, and Richard Moll. The protagonist, played by Katt, moves from the mistake of retreating from his demons (fear) to the mistake of attempting to destroy them, ultimately discovering that the conflict ends only when he musters the faith to stop believing in their power over him. He learns to stand up for himself by refusing to hide, refusing to fight, and refusing to believe that his fears have the power to destroy him.

And that is our challenge: to believe more in ourselves than we believe in the neurotic Bullies who haunt our minds. But the strength of the fear and negativity we will face to do this is tremendous. What we are up against must not be minimized. I believe in the power of positive thinking and in the power of creative visualization, but I have also witnessed the side effects of these techniques when their application is oversimplified.

Forty-two-year-old Monica had been in therapy since she was sixteen, when her parents had taken her to an adolescent alcohol-and-drug rehabilitation program.

"They had no idea what to do with me," Monica told me during our first meeting, "and all these years later, I feel the same way: I don't know what to do with me either."

When I meet with clients who have been in as much therapy as Monica, I am immediately curious about why they are still in therapy. Do they have chronic mental illness (i.e., depression, anxiety, bipolar disorder) or a personality disorder that requires long-term monitoring, medical treatment, and supportive psychotherapy? Do they have a mental illness that has not been accurately diagnosed and treated? Is there an unresolved trauma or loss in their past that has blocked significant progress? Monica did not fit into any of these categories as far as I could tell, but she was definitely stuck.

"How has therapy benefited you in the past?" I asked her.

"I definitely understand myself in ways that I don't think I would without therapy. I feel good about all that I have learned. And this may sound strange, but I enjoy it," Monica said.

"What have you found most helpful in therapy in the past?"

"It always helps just to get things out," she paused, thinking. "But I'm still not happy."

"You're not happy?"

Monica listened to her own words reflected back to her. "Well, no, that's not really true," she said. "I wouldn't say I'm unhappy." Another pause. "But something's not right, something is still missing. I have been in all kinds of therapy, participated in workshops conducted by some of the best-known and well-respected therapists in the world," again pausing, "but I just don't seem to get it right—not for very long at a time anyway."

I asked, "What do you mean by 'get it right'?"

"Well, I know I'm intelligent and, like I told you, I have learned an awful lot about myself, and I do my best to apply what I have learned, but I'm still not happy."

I didn't say anything; Monica recognized what she had said. "I said it again, didn't I? I said 'I'm not happy.' But that's not true."

"You are happy?" I asked.

"No," she said, laughing. "Wow, this is pretty amazing. I've been in therapy all this time, and I can't even decide if I'm happy or not. You must think I'm an idiot."

"No, I definitely don't think you are an idiot," I said, "but this disagreement you seem to be having with yourself about whether you are happy or not does seem important."

I only saw Monica for about a dozen sessions, in which we focused our attention on defining happiness. Just as Kirby had been conflicted about the definition of life, Monica was confused about what determined happiness.

She had ridden the wave of the very popular New Age therapies of the 1980s, adopting a strong spiritual base emphasizing the importance of positive affirmation. The problem, we discovered, was an oversimplified view of such positive thought. In this view if you think positive thoughts, if you visualize and affirm positive realities, if you say "no" to negative thoughts and images, then everything will be just peachy. Conversely, if things are not going your way, if you struggle with relationships or finances or vocational issues, then you must not be thinking right.

I call this "when metaphysics meets codependency." For many of us classic codependents who already believed ourselves to be responsible for negative realities outside our actual power of control, the metaphysical spiritual teachings that we "create our own reality" soon led us to an even more negative view of ourselves. As Monica and I talked this through, I was reminded of my own experiences in this regard. Having read about the importance of demonstrating "prosperity consciousness" by acting "as if" I had already "manifested" what I was "affirming," I proceeded to dig myself into a fair amount of credit-card debt. It turns out that simply repeating a dollar amount over and over every day does not ensure that the check is in the mail. The bills, however, were definitely in the mail.

The inadvertent result of "when metaphysics meets co-dependency" is a tendency to minimize, even to deny, the strength of the obstacles we find in our paths. Another block to progress in personal growth that can be attributed to our "psychotherapeutic age" is our tendency to settle for increased insight and understanding of ourselves, but stop short of doing what we need to do to really manifest change. Valuing insight for its own sake and stopping short of putting it to work is like a football team so impressed with their game plan that they find it unnecessary to show up for the game. "Don't let your insights live with you rent free," the Nutshell says. "Put them to work."

Monica was not only valuing insight for its own sake; she had also developed an almost "magical thinking" about her life. She unrealistically believed that she could virtually pass through the walls she encountered without any more effort than it took to say a positive affirmation. She had unconsciously come to believe that when she was not passing easily through the obstacles of her life, she was doing something wrong, and she began to equate the existence of her obstacles with unhappiness. This reminded me of the weight lifter complaining about how heavy the weights are.

In one session I asked Monica what she thought the purpose of her life was.

"The purpose of my life? So we're going to deal with the easy questions today," she joked.

"Yeah, what could be simpler?" I smiled. "What is the purpose of your life? Just take a guess."

"I don't want to sound overly cliché, but I suppose I believe that I am here to learn . . . and to help others learn."

"Learn what?" I asked.

"Learn about myself I guess. Learn to be a better person. Learn to be less selfish and more generous. Learn about what's important and what's not."

"That sounds good to me," I said. "Now, how do you suppose you go about learning these important lessons?"

"Through my experience, my daily life. I learn when I am paying attention to my daily life. One thing I feel like I know for sure is that being in the present moment—you know, 'Be here now'—is the toughest lesson, and possibly the most important lesson."

"Think about it," I said. "Specifically how do you learn about yourself when you are paying attention?"

"The biggest lessons seem to be learned when I am faced with problems," Monica said.

"Right," I said. "We learn and grow as we identify and confront the obstacles in life. Think about it this way: if the purpose of your life is to learn, the problems or obstacles are your teachers. When you buy into the simplistic idea that positive thinking is the only lesson worth learning, you fall into the unrealistic and unproductive position of believing you should be able to just wish your teachers away."

Monica thought about what I was saying. "When you put it that way, it doesn't make much sense."

I reminded Monica that I was not speaking against the power of positive thinking, but pointing out that when we make the mistake of defining positive thinking as the power to solve problems with the greatest of ease (to transcend problems), we just might be missing out on some important lessons. Somebody once objected to the saying that "adversity makes the man," with the revision of "adversity reveals the man."

A few months after our final session, I received the following e-mail from Monica:

Dear Thom,

Just a note to thank you again for your contribution to my life lessons, and to share one additional insight with you.

I realized that I had equated enlightenment with happiness. So when I was not in a state of enlightenment (as in most of the time), there was that message coming through that I was unhappy.

Who knows what tomorrow will bring, but for today I am affirming (yes, I still do that) that the quest for enlightenment is what points my direction, and that my happiness is determined by whether or not I am walking in that direction.

Monica

None of this is intended to diminish the importance of positive thinking and "prosperity consciousness." I am still affirming my big dollar figures. The difference today is that I pay far less attention to the Bully, telling me how to "fit in" with the metaphysically enlightened ones, and more attention to the Ally, always clear and to the point, simply telling me to not buy something unless I can pay for it. The Ally lacks the intensity and the urgency that characterizes the Bully, but the Ally has something the Bully does not: solutions.

We tend to think of fear as part of the problem rather than part of the solution. It is important to remember that when we listen to the Ally, we are actually listening to the voice of healthy fear. The Ally stands guard and informs us of real dangers, while the Bully works around the clock magnifying and even inventing dangers. Simply put: healthy fear offers us guidance; neurotic fear tries to control us. One of the Nutshells on my wall reads: "Fear is sometimes wisdom and sometimes folly." Knowing the difference is not always easy, but is essential if we intend to live beyond the Bully's control. Can you hear the Ally's voice within you? Listen past the Bully's cluttered rhetoric for the strong and confident voice of your Ally. What do you hear?

Practicing "prosperity consciousness" to the point of accumulating debt and pursuing "enlightenment" only to experience unhappiness are two excellent examples of how we can easily miss the point when we fall for the Bully's convoluted interpretations.

Being unrealistic about the realities of life, whether in the direction of cynicism or naiveté, constitutes one more way to retreat from our fears. When Dorothy directed the personal threats at me and I moved forward, literally leaning into them, I was demonstrating an important first step into the final letter of our acronym map, *responding*. But it is essential that we not make the mistake of oversimplifying or underestimating what will follow. Whether we think of fear as a long-standing bad habit or a well-prepared adversary, the decision to face it and push against it will predictably take us off the sidelines and put us right in the middle of the playing field.

As President Roosevelt prepared America for the pursuit of a world founded on the four freedoms, he undoubtedly knew that what he proposed was not simple, but would take deep commitment from the American people and people all over the world. If we are serious about returning to Roosevelt's vision, that commitment must begin within each of us individually.

CHAPTER TEN

Signing Up
Realities of Roads Less Traveled

*At the start of each day I dread what I face in the race
   that is running outside.
I jump back in bed and cover my head, but that only
   shuts out the light.*

—JERRY JEFF WALKER

SHORTLY AFTER FRANKLIN ROOSEVELT delineated the four essential freedoms in his 1941 speech, Norman Rockwell ensured their place in our national memory by painting his interpretation of each freedom. The paintings were completed in 1943, and reproductions of Rockwell's four freedoms were sold to raise money for the war effort.

Freedom from Fear depicts a mother and father tucking their two children into bed. Safe and sound. Snug as bugs in a rug. What a magnificent image of safety: Mom and Dad tucking us in, keeping watch over us all through the night. Rockwell's scene is ideal; unfortunately, real life is not.

Sixty years beyond President Roosevelt's speech finds us still reaching for the four freedoms: freedom of speech, freedom to worship as we choose, freedom from want, and freedom from fear. Anyone who might think we live in a world providing those just isn't paying attention.

I believe that the fourth freedom is integrally related to the other three. In order to claim our right to free speech, free worship, and freedom from want, we must be willing to do more than merely stake a claim to the fourth freedom; we must accept the responsibility to do whatever it takes to live our lives outside the control of fear. With our acronym map, a ladder to climb down to deeper feelings, and an ever improving ability to distinguish between the Ally and the Bully, we are significantly more prepared to accomplish this.

My life and my work have taught me that freedom from fear has nothing to do with being rid of fear, and everything to do with making conscious, healthy choices about how we will respond in the presence of fear. No one is going to hand us the four freedoms on a silver platter, and I think that is as it should be. Like Monica, I tend to believe that an important part of being human is the challenge to learn from our experience—struggle and all.

I don't believe struggle is the only way we learn, but it is one very effective way. Too often, however, we struggle for no particular reason other than it is what we are used to. What is familiar tends to be automatically associated with safety, even when it is destructive and dangerous. We tend to prefer even a negative certainty over uncertainty. When we accept responsibility for the fourth freedom, we are choosing a different path. Cliché though it is, it is a road less traveled.

I will always remember the wisdom spoken by a client in a group therapy session one day. Mary's head had been downcast as she described the deep sadness and hurt she was experiencing in her life. Finally Mary looked up, tears and mascara running down her cheeks, from red, swollen eyes. She looked directly at me sitting across the room and said, "No wonder this is the road less traveled."

A short silence followed, then I laughed. Then Mary laughed. Then the other group members laughed. It was not laughter that discounted or minimized what Mary was feeling; it was laughter of recognition and identification, laughter that joins us together, laughter that says, "No shit, Sherlock."

The less-traveled roads are more difficult to travel. Certainly they are more challenging. I suppose they are not as well maintained (supported and reinforced by society) as the cultural equivalents to our interstate system. Take the back roads, the scenic route, away from the freeway traffic, and there will be more twists and turns. There will be two-lane highways where we will be slowed down by the farmer and his pickup truck or the even slower tractor, where we have to use good judgment about when to pass the car in front of us and when to practice patience by simply slowing down and enjoying the drive. What an interesting concept: slowing down to enjoy the ride.

Everyone in group therapy that day knew what Mary meant and something of what she was feeling when she said,

"No wonder this is the road less traveled." No one can accurately describe to another what a commitment to personal growth will feel like, but once we have traveled a ways down that road, we feel a sort of bond of recognition with each other. It is important that we celebrate that connection, but avoid the mistake of feeling and expressing this bond as just one more way to be judgmental and arrogant, thinking that we on the road less traveled are something special, something beyond the interstate travelers. In fact, I have discovered that it is best not to assume that I have the capacity to determine what road someone else is traveling at all. This is called humility, and it is a very good thing to keep on hand; it will save considerable energy that we might otherwise spend on evaluating and judging others.

Fear loves judgment, and there is nothing more efficient at plopping us right back into the mainstream traffic as judgment. Fear uses judgment like a carpenter uses a hammer. Consider how it works:

We are afraid of what others will think of us—some we know, many we have not yet met, and even more whom we will never meet. We are afraid of individuals and collections of individuals; their potential criticism terrifies us. But we criticize and condemn those very same people because we think the best defense is a good offense. We judge them to distract ourselves from our fear of them. "You are stupid (or silly, naive, unscrupulous, incompetent, a little off the mark, or evil incarnate)" is easier to think than, "I am afraid of you."

That piece came to me in a meditation after a therapist of mine had encouraged me to consider the relationship between fear and judgment. The words flowed out without effort—an indication to me that the little voice within me had spoken again.

There is no doubt that fear fuels judgment. It always has, and it always will. The only choices we have are whether we will believe what fear tells us and whether we will think, feel, and do as it instructs. "Hurry, hide underneath that table," my fear might tell me, and without giving it a second thought (this entire process is about learning to have second thoughts) I am beneath the table, with my head down. Duck and cover I believe we used to call it.

Learning to recognize the distinctive voice of neurotic fear, the Bully, when it speaks, so that we can disagree or at least disobey, is a lesson that lines the roads less traveled like pine trees in North Carolina or palm trees in Florida.

Using the simple metaphor of fear's two voices, the Ally and the Bully, may not seem like much when someone first encounters it, but the potential impact of this practice cannot be underestimated. Learning to perceive our relationship with fear rather than just having the experience of fear has the power to transform our lives. My client Matthew told me that by maintaining a daily awareness of his neurotic fear messages, he has been able to demote the Bully from "Chairman of the Board" to "Intermittent Pain in the Ass." Kirby's ability to experience the relationships within herself helped her first in a struggle to understand what was happening to her and ultimately to find acceptance and peace at the time of her death. June's Bully remains strong, but she does an excellent job identifying and disobeying his instructions most of the time. She tells me that one of her victories is not letting the Bully keep her from marrying the man she loves.

"I didn't even invite the Bully to the wedding," June said one day.

"So your wedding was Bully free?" I asked.

"No," she said, "he came anyway. I just didn't pay much attention to him."

The ramifications of drastically changing our relationship with fear only begins with the individual benefits. The ripple effect spreads into our communities, from the smallest two-person family to global relations between nations. (Marshall Rosenberg, Ph.D., a clinical psychologist, teacher, and author, writes eloquently about the expansion of this ripple effect in his book *Nonviolent Communication* [1999].)

As I said at the beginning, my work has been predominantly about helping others to seek freedom from fear of the internal tyranny that threatens us. But when we consider the potential for this powerful ripple effect, there is no such clear line of demarcation between internal and external threat. You may be familiar with the phrase "As above, so below," an expression of spiritual congruence. In this case the expression might be "As within, so without," meaning that the internal conditions of our psyches are ultimately reflected in the world around us.

The politician who responds more to the pressures of partisan politics than to the expressed desires of her constituents is not a brave woman. The community member who does not speak out when that same politician betrays his trust is no better. This is not so much a description of cowardice as it is a description of a cultural laziness. We tend to take those paths of least resistance—living by default—until something awakens us to the greater possibilities that conscious choice brings.

I believe there are few, if any, exceptions. Humans are forgetful and easily distracted. We all need to be awakened— our memories jogged—usually multiple times, because we tend to hit the snooze button for just those few more minutes of sleep.

The full potential of the ripple effect is probably beyond what we can imagine, and certainly beyond what we will experience and witness in a lifetime. But we should not allow the limitations of our human nature to stop us from doing our share of the work, beginning at the most personal level. This is not a sermon to rally political involvement. It is an expression of my belief that every time one of us makes peace with something previously unresolved, the ripple effect is activated. By putting our acronym map to work, we can become a better spouse, parent, friend, and community member.

The challenge is to become willing to drop a few stones into the water and see where the ripples take us, knowing once again that even though we do not control the process, we are in charge of our responses. Frequently the ripples take us back in time to discover something about another ripple effect: the effect of our past on our present.

Virginia was four years old when her mother died from cancer. Other than a few photographs, she has no memories of her mom. Her father remarried within eighteen months of his wife's death. Virginia believes that his primary motivation

for remarrying was that his five children "needed a mother."
If this is true, he did not do a very good job choosing a quali-
fied person for the position. Virginia's stepmother was both
verbally and physically abusive to the children, becoming
more a ruler of the home than a parent. Even without memories of her natural mother, Virginia never came to think of
her stepmother as her parent, and except when necessary to
avoid punishment, she consistently refused to call her
"Mother." Since her stepmother's name was Marjorie and
her last name began with the letter *F*, Virginia referred to
her stepmother in therapy sessions as "M.F." The joke was
not lost on me.

Virginia came to therapy with rather vague complaints.
We had met several times before I began to get a handle on
what she was doing in my office and what I might be able to
do to help.

"Jimmy [Virginia's husband] gets mad because he says I
just sort of 'go away' during a conversation. I can tell that he
is really frustrated, but I don't know what I can do about it,"
Virginia said.

"Do you 'go away' as Jimmy says?" I asked her.

"I'm sure I do," she said. "For me, though, it doesn't feel
like going away. I just don't have anything to say."

I was thinking that either Virginia was a naturally quiet
person and that frustrated her husband or she was emotionally shutting down in response to certain cues in their conversations. She did not strike me as a naturally quiet person.
She had been quite articulate in our sessions so far, and I
had not witnessed any behavior that seemed like emotionally

shutting down. Of course, Virginia and I had experienced no conflict in our relationship to this point, and it was a fairly safe bet that if she was shutting down, she was doing that in conversations that involved conflict.

I suggested that Virginia invite Jimmy to one of our sessions, and when he joined us, the three of us fairly quickly identified the "shutdown," as we had begun to call it. We discovered that it happened automatically in response to Jimmy's volume and tone of voice. Predictably, the more frustrated he became, the more irritated he sounded. This ensured Virginia's "shutdown."

The connection between the "shutdown" and the abuse endured from her stepmother was not difficult to make. As a child, Virginia had quickly learned to take the path of least resistance with her stepmother.

"What would be the use of fighting back?" Virginia said. And I could see the defeat in her facial expression and posture.

Virginia had learned to retreat at the first sign of attack, indicated predominantly through voice tone and volume. She had learned this technique so well that she was still automatically using it in her marriage.

I asked Virginia, "When you shut down, or when you do what Jimmy calls 'going away,' where do you go?"

"I never thought about it," she said.

"Let's see what we can find out," I said, beginning a sort of modified ladder technique. "Just say what comes to mind. 'When I shut down, I . . . '"

Virginia completed the first rung on the ladder: "When I shut down, I am safe."

I continued, "I am safe because . . ."

". . . because I have shut down." It is not unusual with this kind of exercise to encounter a loop like this. When I shut down, I am safe. I am safe because I have shut down. The key to getting out of the loop is simple persistence.

"When I am shut down and safe . . . ," I continued.

Virginia was quiet for several seconds, sometimes a sign that someone is giving too much thought to the association. But Virginia was not thinking as much as she was listening. She was listening inwardly to a response that surprised her.

"This is interesting," she said. "I'm not sure what to make of it, but it goes like this: when I am shut down and safe, I am strong." Virginia's voice was unsure, juxtaposing the word "strong" with her tentativeness.

"You are strong," I said, not as a question, but as a declarative statement. I wanted to reflect what she had said back to her, but without the tentativeness.

She picked right up on it. "Yes, I am strong." Virginia sat up a little straighter; she seemed to throw her shoulders back just slightly.

I suggested to Virginia that she close her eyes as a way to help maintain an inward focus. I asked her to tell me about her strength.

With eyes closed, she described her experience. "When I focus on this feeling, or whatever it is, I feel calm. Strangely calm."

"You feel strong and calm?" I asked.

"Well . . . no . . . it's more like the calmness is the strength. Like I'm in a safe place and no one can find me."

Virginia was quiet; then she smiled and said, "I guess Jimmy was right. I do go away."

I wanted Virginia to keep exploring her experience undistracted. I simplified a summary to that point. "When you are scared by potential conflict, you go away to a secret place where no one can find you. And there you feel safe and calm. Is that right?"

"Yes, but there is something else here," Virginia said after reviewing my summary.

"Something else?" I asked. "Like some-thing or some-one else?"

"No," she said, "another feeling—something beyond the strength and the calm."

"What feeling?"

"Anger, I think. But that's not exactly it." I watched Virginia sit on the sofa in my office, with eyes closed, but I imagined her holding this new discovery in her hands, turning it this way and that, examining it, trying to accurately classify the discovery like a geologist with a rock specimen. "It's like a certain attitude—kind of smart aleck . . . "

"If this attitude was a person, what would it be saying?" I asked, trying to help.

Virginia smiled. I could tell she had "heard" an instant answer to my question. "What is it?" I asked.

"Well it's not very nice," she said.

"This is therapy. You don't have to be nice," I assured her.

"F—k you."

"What?" I'm not often caught off guard in therapy sessions anymore, but this took me by surprise.

"F—k you," Virginia repeated. "That's what the attitude says."

Virginia and I discovered what she eventually named her "Quiet Rebel." In the face of her stepmother's harsh—seemingly even malicious—control, Virginia's quiet rebellion had served her well. Specifically, it had helped her remain in possession of her own identity. Virginia's self-esteem sustained considerable damage in the line of her stepmother's fire, but the Quiet Rebel protected her from completely collapsing into believing that she was the person her stepmother portrayed her to be. In one session, Virginia described her Quiet Rebel as a guardian for the more vulnerable aspects of her personality. "She's like a smart, tough big sister," Virginia said.

Such defenses in childhood are often instrumental in psychological, and sometimes physical, survival. As children, we are inherently resourceful in creating ways to reduce the amount and severity of damage done, even when we cannot avoid the detrimental circumstance. We become extremely helpful, accepting responsibility for the well-being of everyone around us; or we become troublemakers, expressing our pain (and the family's pain) through behavioral problems; or we take an approach similar to Virginia's, building a high tolerance for neglect and/or abuse, holding the inevitable pain inside while we outwardly remain very still, not daring to rock the boat.

As she grew into adolescence, Virginia increasingly adopted the identity of the Quiet Rebel. Her philosophy became "stand there and take whatever M.F. had to dish out, pretend contrition or whatever the situation called for, then later do whatever she wanted to do." For Virginia—as for many of us—her childhood survival skills were necessary and highly creative, but were not enough for her to feel genuinely satisfied with her life.

I explained to Virginia that what she had previously thought to be her weakness and cowardice (not standing up to conflict) was better described as strength and courage. At least it was the strength and courage of a child who had lost her mother when she was four years old and who was subsequently placed in the care of an adult who was emotionally not much more mature than a four-year-old herself.

"The strength and courage you need now," I suggested to Virginia, "are different from what you needed as a child. In order to claim your right to be in charge of your own life, it is time to let the Quiet Rebel speak."

"I need to speak up in my marriage. I know that I have to stop 'shutting down' and 'going away' whenever Jimmy seems the slightest bit upset," Virginia said.

"Yes, and you have already started doing that according to what you have been telling me." It is extremely important, and often difficult, to learn to acknowledge progress in personal-growth work, and I wanted to be sure Virginia recognized that she had already begun to change. Interestingly, one early result of Virginia's becoming more assertive at home was that Jimmy had begun some individual therapy of his own to explore, among other things, his tendency to become frustrated so quickly. It does indeed take two to tango.

Because the object of therapy is to heal our psychological wounds from the inside out, I suggested that Virginia write a letter to her stepmother as a gesture symbolic of taking charge of her own life. This kind of therapeutic letter is written to help release pent-up feelings, and I always recommend that the writer make a promise to not send the letter to the addressee. This promise ensures that there is no need for censorship. "Just get some blank paper and let the pen write whatever it wants to write," I said to Virginia.

The result was a letter that represents the real Virginia and her incredible honesty, creativity, and unique sense of humor. Here is what she wrote:

> M.F.:
>
> *Being your stepdaughter is like wearing a pair of ugly, bad-fitting shoes. It doesn't look good, it doesn't feel good, and I have calluses that will probably never go away.*
>
> *Being your stepdaughter has made me feel embarrassed, ashamed, afraid, ugly, dishonest, unimportant, and numb. You managed to belittle, berate, and humiliate me almost to the point of no return. You killed my spirit, burst my bubble, beat me up, and made a pretty good liar out of me.*
>
> *You paralyzed me with your wicked stares. You showed me who was in charge. You kept me in a constant state of fear. You made me forget spontaneous laughter. You helped me build walls all around me that kept me distant emotionally, intellectually, and socially. Because of those walls, I have not been too willing or eager to accept love, learning, or friendship. I haven't lived much; I have just watched as life "happens."*

You were so hell-bent on establishing your dictatorship that casualties didn't matter. I wasn't the only one. We all suffered damage under your reign.

You made me so afraid. Not just of you . . . I began to fear much that life has to offer. Precious things like intimacy. Simple things like autonomy. On the one hand, I regret all the years I lived that way. On the other, I rejoice that I no longer do.

When I think about my adolescence, I feel an overwhelming sense of waste. I didn't know much, care much, smile much, or do much that was positive. My body was present, but my soul was long gone.

Too bad you wasted so much time on threats and rage. Too bad you focused on mean, belittling comments. Tragic that you took away my chances for a happy childhood.

In closing, I'll tell you this: I blame you for most of the negatives in my life, and credit you for little good. But I am happy and proud to say that in spite of you, I survived. I can laugh out loud. I can look up instead of down. And I am grateful every day for the happy and healthy family I helped to create.

Virginia

P.S. My therapist made me write this letter.

The blame that Virginia places with her letter is not about harboring a resentment toward her stepmother. In fact, by stating her opinion so clearly—with little concern for self-help political correctness—Virginia is taking a giant step toward letting go of her resentments. The Nutshell on my wall relevant to this reads: "Blame is a good place to visit; you just don't want to live there."

Robert Subby, in his book *Lost in the Shuffle* (1987), says it even better. Subby writes, "As children we are victims; as adults we are volunteers." The challenge is to make a commitment to see the truth as clearly as it can be seen, to make no excuses for our parents or other caregivers during our childhood, and no excuses for ourselves in adulthood.

Franklin Roosevelt's fourth inaugural address was the briefest in American history. In that short 573-word speech, given less than three months before he died, President Roosevelt said:

> We can gain no lasting peace if we approach it with suspicion and mistrust—or with fear. We can gain it only if we proceed with the understanding and the confidence and the courage which flow from conviction.

These words hold true for us today, whether we are talking about our place in the global community or contemplating the internal workings of our complex human mind.

We do have a right to live beyond fear's control, but with that right comes the responsibility to *face, explore, accept,* and *respond* consciously and proactively to the truth that we will discover when we do not run away. These roads are less traveled because they are difficult roads along which we will be repeatedly confronted with the simple human fear of stepping outside our own comfort zone. Whether that means standing up consistently to the Bully within us, or speaking the truth in our marriages, or traveling back through time to rescue ourselves from abusive circumstances, it must be done. How else will we learn?

How do you feel about confronting your Bully? Can you see yourself making the conscious decision to take the next exit to discover the less traveled, but far more scenic, side roads of your life? Does the thought scare you a little?

Don't forget that some of the fear you will experience is perfectly healthy. The Ally, always less verbose than the Bully, doesn't pull any punches. The Ally tells us that it won't be easy, but is also the first to tell us that our investment is a good one. The Ally speaks to us from the perspective of what I think of as the one legitimate fear. That's right, I said there is ultimately only one legitimate fear. In the simplest terms, I call it "the fear of missing the point."

Most of us can agree that it is not that we live, but how we live that matters most. At least we believe this with our brains and our words. But it is so easy to become caught up in our day-to-day lives, and in the circumstances beyond our control, and consequently drift from our own personal value systems. The Bully is always available to help with this.

When we speak of love, but act from fear, a split in our value system occurs. When the Bully successfully scares us away from our dreams and plans, we feel the pain. The Ally knows about that pain and is there to warn us—to scare us a little.

"Don't forget what is important," the Ally says with quiet confidence.

Unlike the Bully, the Ally respects that we will make our own choices. The Ally does not insist that we listen, but simply makes wisdom available to us. It is our job to pay attention, and our job to decide that the one legitimate fear—acting outside our personal value system—is bigger than the thousands and thousands of little fears the Bully barrages us with every day.

Frequently in therapy I ask clients to write letters like the one Virginia wrote to her stepmother. They are letters to help declare independence from the past. As a follow-up to Virginia's letter, I was about to suggest that she write another letter, this time to the neurotic fear that had previously kept her on the sidelines of life. As I considered this assignment for her, I looked back at what she had written and realized that by removing only two minor references to her stepmother, Virginia had already written a powerful declaration of independence from her fear.

Read it again with the small changes.

Dear Bully:

Being under your control is like wearing a pair of ugly, bad-fitting shoes. It doesn't look good, it doesn't feel good, and I have calluses that will probably never go away.

Being your loyal subject has made me feel embarrassed, ashamed, afraid, ugly, dishonest, unimportant, and numb. You managed to belittle, berate, and humiliate me almost to the point of no return. You killed my spirit, burst my bubble, beat me up, and made a pretty good liar out of me.

You paralyzed me with your wicked stares. You showed me who was in charge. You kept me in a constant state of fear. You made me forget spontaneous laughter. You helped me build walls all around me that kept me distant emotionally, intellectually, and socially. Because of those walls, I have not been too willing or eager to accept love, learning, or friendship. I haven't lived much; I have just watched as life "happens."

You were so hell-bent on establishing your dictatorship that casualties didn't matter. I wasn't the only one. We all suffered damage under your reign.

You made me so afraid. Not just of you . . . I began to fear much that life has to offer. Precious things like intimacy. Simple things like autonomy. On the one hand, I regret all the years I lived that way. On the other, I rejoice that I no longer do.

When I think about my adolescence, I feel an overwhelming sense of waste. I didn't know much, care much, smile much, or do much that was positive. My body was present, but my soul was long gone.

Too bad you wasted so much time on threats and rage. Too bad you focused on mean, belittling comments. Tragic that you took away my chances for a happy childhood.

In closing, I'll tell you this: I blame you for most of the negatives in my life, and credit you for little good. But I am happy and proud to say that in spite of you, I survived. I can laugh out loud. I can look up instead of down. And

I am grateful every day for the happy and healthy family I helped to create.

Virginia

I didn't need to give Virginia the additional assignment, so I will give it to you. Write a letter to your Bully. Make it your declaration of independence.

CHAPTER ELEVEN

Beyond the Wall
Living the Courageous Life

Insist on yourself; never imitate.

—RALPH WALDO EMERSON

ON A SUNDAY MORNING in the spring of 1959, a young black woman—a teenager really—stepped into the sanctuary of the all-white Park Street Methodist Church in Atlanta, Georgia. Two ushers moved quickly toward her with the obvious intent to escort her out of the building. The general policy of the church was for ushers to discourage the attendance of anyone whose presence might have a "disturbing influence" on the congregation.

The forty-year-old pastor leading the service paused for what must have seemed an eternity, but was in fact more like five seconds.

"This is God's house," the pastor said. "Everyone is welcome to worship here."

The ushers reluctantly stepped away, and the young woman seated herself. Later in the service she took communion at the altar, kneeling between two white girls.

If you are in the market for a role model for facing fear, there are several very courageous people in this story. I do not know the name of the young black woman, but would love to meet and thank her for the strength she demonstrated that day. I am privileged to have known the pastor, Reverend Leon Smith. Thirty years later, Leon was my therapist for a time, and later he was my colleague and my friend. He has always been a role model for courage.

When Leon died at age eighty-two, his son Mark shared with me a letter written by a woman who was in attendance at Park Street Church that day.

> *Dear Mark,*
>
> *I'm sure my letter is one of many you and your family will receive as people hear about your dad's death. I was a teenager when Leon was pastor of Park Street Church in West End. How lucky that was for me! His integrity, his warmth, his humor, his intellect, and his social conscience made such an impact on my life and the lives of those in my generation of young people.*
>
> *I remember well the incident about the black woman attending Park Street Church. I even remember that it was Carrell Ann Larmore and Julie Winn who knelt by her side during communion. I have never been prouder of my home church than at that moment. During those days of racial*

unrest, I lost faith in many Park Streeters of my parents'
generation. Your dad, however, made it clear that not all
people of that age group were filled with bigotry and hatred.
With deepest sympathy for your loss,
Judy Thomas Nobles

The two young women, Carrell Ann Larmore and Julie
Winn, who knelt beside the young black woman that day, are
also role models for courage. Carrell Larmore also wrote on
the occasion of Leon's death, and Mark shared her letter
with me:

Dear Mark,

It was with great sadness that I read in the Atlanta
papers of your father's death. What a special man, and
your mom a special woman, and the two of them a special
couple.

I was one of the Park Street teenagers when your fam-
ily was there. I was home on vacation from Duke the day
the young Spelman student came in. Your father handled
that situation with such courage and grace. I was on the
same pew with her, and at communion, stepped back and
let her go down between Julie Winn and myself, rather
than subject her to walk next to the angry people behind
us. Your father's lead gave me the courage to take my own
first step for civil rights. I later became very involved in
the civil rights movement as I returned to Duke.

Carrell Larmore (Dammann)

I am certain that the majority of the other people attending the Park Street worship service that day were not bad or
evil people. Maybe it's not even fair to characterize them as
cowards. But there were certainly many there that day who
did not move past their wall built solid with fear-mortar in
order to act with strength and integrity. Had I been there, I
would of course like to think that I too would have acted
with courage, but I cannot know that. Imagine the courage
that would have us take a stand in the face of racism today
and multiply that by a thousand—at least. That is some
measure of the courage shown that day at the Park Street
Church in Atlanta, Georgia.

Did these people act in the way they did because it came
naturally to them? Were Leon's and Carrell's and Julie's and
especially the young black woman's first instincts to take a
stand? How much fear did they overcome to be the people
they were that day, to act in such a way that more than forty
years later I am telling you their story? I don't know the
answers to these questions, and ultimately it doesn't matter.
What matters is they did what they needed to do to act con-
gruently with personal value systems that included belief in
equality of all people and belief, in this particular instance,
in one of the cornerstones of this country, one of President
Roosevelt's delineated four freedoms: the right to worship as
one chooses.

Our actions determine who we are. Intention counts,
but is a poor substitute for self-definition. Be careful with
this idea; be sure to notice that it does *not* say, "The outcome of our actions determines who we are." Many vari-

ables affect outcome, and although we certainly influence outcome, we seldom control it. Perfectionists become paralyzed because they believe the opposite: that results are all that count.

Often we do not know—and might never know—the ultimate results of our actions. It is a mistake to measure only the immediate consequence. I am sure that the courageous people at the Park Street Church that spring day in 1959 did not see any discernible change in racist attitudes, but the ripple effect of their actions joined with increasing numbers of many ripple effects over the next years to become a massive wave in the form of the civil rights movement.

My college friend Sarah told me in 1975 that if I could care about a person as much as I seemed to care about alcohol, I might have a chance for a successful relationship. I didn't stop drinking for another eleven years, but Sarah's words never left me. And they never stopped being true. This is the ripple effect of telling the truth.

That is the essence of this book: telling the truth, speaking up with words and deeds. My good friend Evelyn Barkley Stewart, author of *Life with the Panic Monster,* says that when we give voice to our fears—tell the truth about our vulnerabilities—we are instantly less likely to be acting out of fear. Evelyn inspired this Nutshell: "Tell on your fears. It's the appropriate use of tattling."

To practice the NO FEAR motto recommended by the wise little voice in my head, I must speak up. It will not do for me to keep who I am a secret from the rest of the world. The big challenge for me, and for you, is to represent ourselves well, to learn all about who we want to be, and then go out there and be that person to the very best of our inherently imperfect abilities.

I had the opportunity several years ago to give a series of lectures to some of the employees of the Jack Daniels Corporation (Brown-Forman, Inc.). This was especially intriguing to me as a recovering alcoholic. Since my presentation included references to my alcoholism, I told them to please understand that I had nothing against their product.

"In fact," I told the Jack Daniels employees, "I like your product verrrrrry much—and therein lies the problem.

"But I am a fair-minded man," I told them, "and there came a time when I knew that I had already had my lifetime share of Jack Daniels, and the only right thing to do was to leave some for others."

During the lecture series I referred not only to my battle with alcoholism, but also to being diagnosed and treated for depression and specifically focused on my history of excessive self-criticism and my long-term relationship with neurotic fear. I never want to overshadow my message by telling too many stories about myself, but I insist on being very clear that an important part of my claim to credibility comes from personal experience, not just from professional training and experience.

At the close of one of the Jack Daniels lectures, a woman who looked to be in her fifties came up to me, shook my hand, and said with complete sincerity, "I just want to thank you for being so messed up."

In response I laughed, but replied with equal sincerity, "You're welcome."

I knew what the woman meant. She was thanking me for being "so messed up" and being willing to talk about it. Frequently people tell me that they feel relieved to know that what they have been experiencing for a lifetime is not unusual. Remember, we live in a culture that perpetuates the "myth of singularity," that ridiculous notion that we experience—or at least should experience—our consciousness as a unified thought process. When people hear that, in fact, we all have busy committees at work between our ears, that this is the norm, there is great relief for two primary reasons. First, it is just nice to know you aren't crazy and, second, understanding that multiplicity is the true nature of human consciousness introduces brand-new hope for improved self-esteem and success in life. A very popular Nutshell on my wall reads: "We all talk to ourselves; we just need to get better at it."

Consider the following monologue:

I am afraid, I am weak for being afraid, I am a chicken. It is normal to be afraid, and being afraid doesn't make me a chicken. I am weak and definitely a chicken. I am confused, I am weak, I am not that abnormal, I am normal, I am the furthest thing from normal. I am pitiful. Besides being weak, I am crazy—just listen to my crazy thoughts. I think I'm okay, no real problem here. I am the poster child for problems. I'm pretty sure I'm fine. Weak. I don't think so.

The essence of what I teach clients, audiences, and readers that has the potential to change everything can be found—you guessed it—on my therapy-room wall. A couple of Nutshells apply. One reads "It's not the thought that counts; it's your relationship to the thought." Another puts it more concisely: "Everything is relationship."

When we translate the previous monologue into relationship terms by identifying two distinct voices, it reads like this:

Me: I am afraid.

Critic: You are weak for being afraid. You are a chicken.

Me: It is normal to be afraid, and being afraid does not make me a chicken.

Critic: No. You are weak, and definitely a chicken.

Me: I am confused.

Critic: Sure, you are confused because you are weak.

Me: I don't think this is unusual; I'm not that abnormal. In fact, what I am experiencing is normal.

Critic [Laughs]: You are the furthest thing from normal. You are pitiful. Besides being weak, you are crazy— just listen to your crazy thinking.

Me: No, I think I'm okay. These "crazy thoughts" are just you insulting me. No real problem here.

Critic: No problem?! You are the poster child for problems!

Me: I'm pretty sure that I'm fine.

Critic: Weakling!

Me: No, I don't think so.

(Notice that the critical voice in this dialogue does not change its opinion, and does not have to change its opinion in order for me to feel better.)

Transforming the monologue into dialogue makes a couple of interesting and very important differences. Most obviously, it becomes less confusing; our minds don't feel that they need to go back and forth trying to track the thoughts and make some sense of the contradictions. In the monologue, the contradictions themselves represent at least confusion and sometimes a sense of (or fear of) insanity. In the dialogue, the contradictions are not only understandable; we see that the difference of opinion is actually the purpose of the thought process. When the critical voice is present, we need to have these conversations. Otherwise, we will fall into agreement with the criticism literally without giving it a second thought.

If clarity is the most obvious difference made by the translation to dialogue, I think the most important difference is this: when we can perceive our central identities as separate from certain lines of thought (self-criticism about fear and the meaning of fear in this case), we have someone to root for; there emerges a hero to our story. Read back over both the monologue and the dialogue. After reading each one, ask yourself whose side you are on.

The dialogue version creates the opportunity for us to get on our own side, to be our own advocate. This is especially necessary for those of us who have spent many years so identified with self-criticism and internal threats that we have come to accept the negative lines of thought as objective reality. Often, for us to speak the truth, we have to begin with these internal disagreements—essentially speaking at least two very different "truths." The fear that blocks us here is the fear of opening the proverbial can of worms or the mythological Pandora's box.

I remember that Kirby and I wondered during one of her therapy sessions if by practicing the dialogue technique we might have inadvertently empowered the aspect of her personality that defined living as getting beyond physical life. After thinking it through, we both agreed with what I still believe today: that by translating thought process into dialogue, we are not creating anything that is not already in existence. And by shining the spotlight of awareness on the internal conflict, the aspect of the personality that stands to gain strength, credibility, and power is what I have come to think of as the central identity, referred to in some of my previous writings as the Decision Maker.

To move beyond the understandable fear of the can of worms or Pandora's box, we need only return to our acronym map. For example:

Face the fear: I am afraid that once I begin to pay closer attention to my internal conflict, I will feel worse rather than better, that I will be beginning something I will later regret, and that I will be beginning something that I will not be able to successfully finish.

Explore the fear: Applying the ladder technique to the fear described above:

"I am afraid of feeling worse and of failing."

"If I feel worse and if I fail, then I will lose what hope I have left."

"If I lose what hope I have left, I'll be finished and have to resign myself to live in emotional pain."

[That is actually far enough down the ladder to be very productive, but I like to go down another rung or two below that. It can be helpful.]

"If I am finished and resigned to live in emotional pain, I will have realized my greatest fears of being useless and alone."

(I am intrigued by how frequently the ladder leads to fears of aloneness and/or being without purpose. Rather than thinking of this in pathological terms, I believe this speaks powerfully to our human need for community and our spiritual need to make a difference.)

Accept the fear: These are my fears. They are not the facts, and they are not an accurate prophecy of what will result when I choose to focus more on my internal conflict. I do not need to change my fears. They are what they are, but they do not have the authority to stop my forward progress.

Respond to the fear: I acknowledge that by deciding to focus directly on my internal conflict, I will be choosing to move into a mental and emotional space of confusion and increased fear. I know that it will likely become darker before the dawn. But I do not believe that my greatest fears (uselessness and aloneness) will come to pass, and, in fact, I believe that these things threaten me only if I do not choose to proceed in this personal-growth work. And acknowledging that I am an imperfect human without the power of prophecy, by choosing to do this personal-growth work I am accepting the risk that my fears may be true. I do not believe they are true, but I am willing to risk it. The value of this twofold response—diminishing the credibility of internal threats and simultaneously accepting the risk that they are true—cannot be overemphasized.

One additional technique that can be enlisted to help with this is the "If–Then" strategy. Here is how it works: you make a list of specific fears in any given situation, and then you address each fear, one at a time, by pretending that it has actually happened. In response to each fear, create a specific plan for how you will respond in a healthy and productive manner. For example, if the fear is losing your job, then make a plan for what to do when you lose your job: "If I lose my job, it will hurt and be very scary, but I don't have to panic. I have a list of friends and associates who will be willing to help me find employment. I might even find a better job."

For obvious reasons this technique has been criticized as being negative and counterproductive. And it would be if the fear scenario becomes the focal point. The opposite is intended, however. By making a realistic and specific plan to deal effectively with each fear on the list, we free ourselves from having to pay attention to the internal threatening, "You're going to be sorry" messages.

Fear says, "If you do what this idiot, Rutledge, tells you, you will surely lose your job, and your husband will leave you."

You of course feel the tug in your gut, for these are important elements in your life, but to the fear you respond, "I don't think so, but if so, I have made plans to handle the fallout."

As I hope you have seen throughout this book, even the most effective techniques do not relieve us of the feelings of fear. Fear is one of the universal experiences that connect us all as human beings. Certainly, how each of us experiences and responds to fear can be unique, but the bigger truth is that there are only two kinds of people when it comes to fear: those who acknowledge feeling afraid and those who are lying (to themselves and/or to others). Are there rare exceptions to this? Maybe, but they are definitely a minority.

The lesson I hope you will take from *Embracing Fear* and apply on a daily basis is the practice of tuning into your inner committee and distinguishing between healthy and neurotic fear—the Ally and the Bully. I believe how we respond to these two is what determines the meaning of our lives. This idea is beautifully expressed in the Albert Brooks film *Defending Your Life*, in which Brooks and costar Meryl Streep play characters recently deceased who are taken to "Judgment City," where they undergo a complete life review to determine what the next step will be in each soul's journey. The determining factor, it turns out, is how people responded to fear during their lifetime. If you haven't seen

the movie, definitely rent it. You will be completely enter-
tained and simultaneously feel as though you have been
through an excellent therapy session.

How we respond to fear determines how effectively we
will face and push through the walls in our lives. Remember,
fear is the mortar that holds a wall together. To weaken the
mortar we must move directly toward our fears, climb down
our ladders, and put our acronym map to work. When we do
these things, it is certain that we will break through to the
other side.

Return to the wall visualization for a moment, remembering the closing lines that ask about life beyond the wall:

> What is it like on this side of the wall? The sky, the
> ground, the air around you—what is it like? What do you
> see? What do you hear? And what do you feel?
>
> And what's that in the distance?

In my workshops the final question evokes a broad range
of responses—everything from confusion to frustration to
delight. What do you see in the distance? Look closely
enough and you will see it. Maybe it is towering right in front
of you, or maybe it is on the distant horizon, or somewhere in
between, but it will be there. You guessed it: another wall. It's
life, not an obstacle standing between you and life. Each wall
is a teacher, and we are the students. Whether we are willing
students or not is always our choice, but we will not be given
the option to live without walls, any more than we will be
able to place an order for a calm, serene life—hold the fear.

The work of facing our walls and the fear that holds them together is precisely what we are here to do.

When I walked across the campus of my alma mater and the little voice spoke to me—"Let's look at what happens when fear is in charge"—I had no idea that I had begun a new book. From where I sit now I can see that was exactly what was happening. It was time to write about the most central theme of all personal-growth work: fear. As with every project I have so far undertaken, I have experienced the material as I have written it. Stephen King says that he is not only the author of his books, but he is also each book's first reader. I know exactly what Mr. King means. Writing *Embracing Fear* has been one more occasion for me to *face, explore, accept,* and *respond* to my fears and to my next walls. I have done my best to practice what I teach, often using the very techniques described in this book to get past a newly encountered block.

As usual, I have discovered my Bully trying to wedge his foot in the door, trying to tell me what my greatest fears should be. But no matter how often I will fall for the Bully's little tricks, slipping back into my own neurosis, I am committed to maintaining my connection to what I know is, and should be, my greatest fear: the fear of not listening to the wisdom within me, the fear of not following my heart.

It only recently occurred to me that the wise little voice within me, the one who taught me the NO FEAR motto, is none other than the Ally. My own healthy fear is the wise voice that will guide me past the control of the Bully. My own healthy fear will help me remember what is important and will remind me to stay away from dangerous perfectionism. In fact, my own healthy fear recently wrote this new Nutshell for my office wall: "Continual fear of making a mistake is a terrible mistake."

The Ally tells me now to add something to the NO FEAR motto. The little addendum to the campus lecture says, "Take the risk. You're worth it."

I say the same to you.

Thom's Nutshells

1. Self-Saboteur's Motto: you cannot lose what you do not have.
2. Heart and mind work best as equal partners.
3. All things in turmoil in and around you are evidence that you are still alive.
4. Growth always moves from the inside out.
5. Courage is to fear as light is to darkness.
6. The human condition is one of chronic forgetfulness.
7. The difference between knowledge and wisdom is experience.
8. To be addicted to control is to be endlessly out of control.
9. Hope and fear are traveling companions.
10. Don't waste your dissatisfaction; use it as fuel.
11. Humility is the awareness that I am neither better nor worse than anyone else.
12. Arrogance can only exist where genuine self-love does not.

13. God flunks no one, but he sure does give lots of retests.

14. Hear with your ears, rather than your fears.

15. Seek simplicity. Simplicity works.

16. Victims believe how they are doing is determined by what happens to them; nonvictims believe how they are doing is determined by how they respond to what happens to them.

17. I reserve the right to disagree with myself.

18. Measure strength according to willingness instead of willpower.

19. Forget about finding the right answers; just make a list of some very good questions.

20. I think uncertainty is the nature of life . . . but I can't be sure.

21. Be in charge of your life. Forget about being in control.

22. Always move toward your demons; they take their power from your retreat.

23. Don't let your insights live with you rent free. Put them to work.

24. Fear is sometimes wisdom and sometimes folly.

25. Blame is a good place to visit; you just don't want to live there.

26. Tell on your fears. It's the appropriate use of tattling.

27. We all talk to ourselves; we just need to get better at it.

28. It's not the thought that counts; it's your relation-
    ship to the thought.

29. Everything is relationship.

30. Continual fear of making a mistake is a terrible
    mistake.

Acknowledgments

NONE OF THE BOOKS I have written would exist without two groups of people: the therapists, healers, and friends who have helped me over the past twenty years to "go sane" and the clients who have trusted me to help them do the same. My gratitude to all of you is constant. I especially want to thank the clients and workshop participants whose stories are represented in these pages, including "Virginia" for allowing me to include your letter verbatim.

Embracing Fear in particular would not exist without Oriah Mountain Dreamer; my agent, Joseph Durepos; and my editor at Harper San Francisco, Gideon Weil. Thank you, Oriah, for the invitation to the party. Thank you, Joe, for your wisdom, guidance, and sense of humor. Thank you, Gideon, for making the editing process a valuable education and all about support.

Thank you to Jerry Lincecum for bringing me home to Austin College, the trip that became the catalyst for this book; to Scott Weiss for escorting me into the Macintosh world; to Jay and Vicki Tyler and Kristy Seagle for reading and responding to the manuscript in installments; to Carrell Dammann and Judy Nobles for permission to share your letters; to Jana

Stanfield for permission to include your wonderful song lyrics; to Peter Shockey for the stamp of approval; and to Kristin Beck for finding me in the first place. Thank you to Jennifer Schaefer for your expert assistance in reading, revising, and organizing the manuscript and for your limitless enthusiasm for this project.

Thank you is really not enough for my wife, Dede Beasley. I appreciate your not running the other direction when you see me coming with the next chapter in hand. But most of all, I thank you for being such a wise, patient, and fun lab partner in this big science project we call life.

And always, thank you to Silven and the boys for delivering—right on time.